BEYOND THE BOOKS

Francis Russell Hart

BEYOND
THE BOOKS

*Reflections on Learning
and Teaching*

Ohio State University Press • Columbus

Excerpt from Robyn Davidson, *Tracks* (New York: Pantheon, 1981) is reprinted by permission of Pantheon Books, a division of Random House, Inc.

Quotations from Terry Eagleton, *Literary Theory: An Introduction*, are copyright © 1983 by Terry Eagleton and reprinted by permission of the University of Minnesota Press.

Quotations from Martin Esslin, *An Anatomy of Drama* (London: Temple Smith, 1976), are reprinted by permission of Curtis Brown Group Ltd.

Library of Congress Cataloging-in-Publication Data
Hart, Francis Russell.
    Beyond the books—reflections on learning and teaching / Francis Russell Hart.
       p.   cm.
    Bibliography: p.
    Includes index.
    ISBN 0–8142–0485–6 (alk. paper)
    1. Literature—Study and teaching (Higher) I. Title.
PN59.H36 1989
807′.11—dc19   89-2846
                                      CIP

The job of the teacher, as I see it, is to teach students, not how to draw, but how to learn to draw. They must acquire some real method of finding out facts for themselves, lest they be limited for the rest of their lives to facts the instructor relates.

—Kimon Nicolaides

The challenge of college teaching consists of the concerted effort of every faculty member to reveal the organic relation between the material of his subject and the seminal concepts of both his discipline and others.

—Robert H. Gurland

Put off by confusion, he was about to flee particle physics when Dr. Richard P. Feynman, a Nobel laureate, came to Cornell and taught a course on the subject. "He made complete fun of the ridiculous problems of field theory. And I thought, My God, maybe I'm right. Maybe there's a reason I don't understand this stuff." That experience became a turning point in my development.

—William J. Broad

CONTENTS

PREFACE

What Do We Want?

This is not a book about Education in America, about Cultural Illiteracy, or about the ambiguous educational legacy of the oft-bashed 1960s. Rather, it is a personal study of what we teachers do, what happens in our classrooms, and why. It is written for teachers and would-be teachers—chiefly, but not exclusively, of literature. Teaching and learning are fundamentally interdisciplinary, and I share the discomfort some others feel with current notions of "literature" as a special, self-referential kind of writing. Of course the strangeness of literature is part of its power and part of what we must teach, but I feel more at home with the older (in some quarters newer) notion of "letters"—a cultural activity and social institution of many forms.

The book has been occasioned by recent years of work: observations of, consultations and seminars with, numerous teachers in various fields who sought advice about their teaching; and draws on my own thirty-five years of "thrashing about" in numerous courses, some literary, some interdisciplinary, on all university levels. It enacts the efforts of one irredeemably pragmatic teacher to think theoretically about our options of purpose and method. It is intended to offer what teachers may need and want in order to teach better, through understanding better what we do and why. What do teachers want?

My work as a leader of faculty seminars has revealed wants of three kinds, and all are legitimate. (1) *Therapeutic.* We want support and encouragement in weathering frustration, weariness, staleness. We are disturbed by conflicting commitments, reluctant and unprepared students, wavering standards, and institu-

ix

tional defects. Our teaching can be studied and strengthened only in the face of such facts. But this is not a book of institutional diagnosis. It can offer only companionship (books used to be prized for being "companionable") and measured optimism. My own students of recent years may well be woefully uninformed about canons and civilizations, but they remain far more interesting and sophisticated than their predecessors. (If your ears are offended by a fairly upbeat note, listen no further.) (2) *Tactical.* We want help with problem-solving. We yearn for quick-fixes—nuts, bolts, and Band-Aids, new tricks of the trade. I don't blame us, but quick-fixes are few; so this is not a book of repairs and first-aid—although it is filled with tactical suggestions. (3) *Theoretical.* Some of us—though not enough—want a fuller understanding of learning and teaching, of what we teach and why. But theory is useless here unless wedded to tactical performance and therapeutic support. Tactics in isolation mean little and lead nowhere. Therapy is sterile unless grounded in enlightenment and renewal. We need to realize the interdependence of all three wants.

The dialectical relation of theory and performance is one of the book's themes—theory of literature, yes, but also (and more important) theory of learning and teaching. The orders in which students learn must shape the designs of our courses, and these in turn must dictate the styles of teaching we adopt. This is a second pervasive theme. A third follows from the second and is best expressed in my excerpt from the great art teacher, Kimon Nicolaides (I call it the Kimon Rule): whatever we teach, either we teach students *how to learn* or our teaching comes to a dead end. A fourth theme responds to a basic change or development in our sense of our field. We know of this change, accept it, but are uncertain what to do about it. Let me explain.

At present the theoretical situation of literature is, to say the least, complicated. Its place in the curriculum has evolved; teachers of various fields use literary texts without being sure how to do so, while humanities faculties wonder anxiously whether and how the study of literature can survive. Literary theory outstrips the capacity (sometimes the willingness) of many teachers to understand or apply it. My colleagues at a young urban university with a large literature major (over six hundred) are unusually bright and dedicated; but when I asked in a survey, "Has recent literary theory affected the way you teach?" a majority said, "No." Some claimed they had barely scratched the surface; others had "been there" but were scornful of or bored by what they had found. A few have lived in the hope that these "fads" would go away, but they have not. Of those who responded positively, Charles Knight summed up best what the effects might be: a new awareness of the nature of discourse, a new interdisciplinary emphasis, a new sense of the "significance of my students' responses to literary works," a new dimension of social history.

In part, he was articulating a shift felt vaguely but strongly by almost all. To the question, "Can literature be taught historically?" most answered, "Yes"; and unusually honest Fred Willey replied, "Oh, boy, I doubt it," then revised to, "Sure 'history' can be taught, if we're sure of what it is." Here was the major change. Half of us had always seen it this way; half have come to see it more. Our growing commitment is to teaching literature not just as "aesthetic object" but also as (what we variously call) "social product," "cultural artifact," "imaginative reconfiguration of biographical and social life around the writer," which reflects "the state of the language and what's going on in the world." We all would seem to agree with Terry Eagleton: "It is not a question of debating whether 'literature' should be related to 'history' or not: it is a question of different readings of history itself" (209).

The problem is not whether; the problem is how. One of my colleagues (Pamela Annas) hints at how she does it: she teaches the "climate of reception," the historicity of reading, the historicity of our students when they read. Another (Susan Horton) predicts we will be "thrashing around" for a decade figuring out the "how." I have learned much from both—as I hope the book may show. At any rate, my fourth theme is our "thrashing around."

Some causes of our thrashing are suggested by two other results of my informal survey: "If literature must be taught historically, is it a historical discipline?" Replies reveal a problem or two. The word "discipline" puzzles some and unnerves others.

Even so, a sizable majority of my friends replied, "Yes, ours is a discipline." Discipline of *method?* For some it still means simply "what critics do." For others, it refers to the disciplines we share with many fields: rigor and clarity of reasoning, documentation, etc. Discipline of *standards?* What do we value and how do we evaluate? The replies were chiefly formal or aesthetic. Almost no one cited standards extrinsic to linguistic and aesthetic quality. The answers have little to do with our new commitments to historical and cultural teaching. How can we teach historically if we recognize only ahistorical values?

The Whats and Hows make sense only in light of our values. Why is literary study a desirable, even a mandatory, part of liberal education? I recalled the familiar old humane justifications: to cultivate intellectual powers, to strengthen and enlarge humane insight and sympathy, to provide unique perspectives on history and society—and asked my friends, could they endorse any? I anticipated (even hoped for) many responses like Martha Collins's eloquent, "Q: Why do you like literature? A: Because it is one of the most thoroughly engaging and integrating pleasures I know." Instead, I was surprised at how many said of my catalog (in effect), "All or most of the above." But most emphasized a more modest goal: to make Better Readers. Our problem in defining this goal is matter for later chapters. A few emphasized the other pole, the maker of the text. They seek an awareness of the powers of art in language, of how *homo significans* uses words to make sense, of the potency of the artist as shaper.

The two poles of reader and maker are not in conflict. What moves us is the fear that both matter less and less. We want something to be kept alive in our students; we are passers-on, and this more than anything makes us teachers. How, then, can our passings-on be most alive?

When it comes to answers, we feel some conflict. If (as I believe) my friends are representative, we have two wants in the literary curriculum: (1) we want to "beef up" our introductory courses; (2) we want more "structure" in the major program. (Even some well-meaning folks get caught up in Sixties-Bashing.)

But we have trouble agreeing on what "beefing up" is appropriate and what "structure" makes sense. This book is intended far
less to argue for certain answers, far more to build a context for
seeking them. In the interests of introductory candor, though, let
me outline a program I believe many of us might endorse:

1. One introductory course, "Literature and the Reader";
2. One introductory course, "Authors as Makers in Their
   Worlds";
3. One course in a literary form (narrative, poem, play);
4. One course in a mode (tragedy, comedy, satire, fantasy, etc.);
5. One course in a past epoch or alien cultural context;
6. One course in an author (or pair of authors);
7. One course in the language;

8–10. Electives

Such a program assumes that teaching literature aims at
learning to learn; that we want to develop an understanding of
complementary but distinct approaches or perspectives; that a
"major" should be introduced to all of these. But any such structure matters only insofar as teachers understand that different
perspectives call for different course designs and pedagogies. My
first chapter identifies our general options—the options of teachers in all academic areas.

Chapter 1 sketches a theoretical framework synthesized from
models of learning and teaching; without it, we cannot understand our options. Chapter 2 confronts such a framework with
what actually happens in a college class, any class. Chapters 3
and 4 address the problem of beginnings: where and how can literary learning begin? In chapters 5 and 6, we move to what many
of us see as our most urgent problem: how to teach literature contextually—historically, culturally. In most of these chapters, my
examples emphasize narrative fiction—what most of us do, what
(alas) many students think of as the "whole story." In chapters 7
and 8, we focus on teaching the "other forms," and finally, in
chapter 9, I discuss what it means nowadays to teach an Author.

The book is designed as a whole, but do not expect a single linear "argument." You can read it in parts, according to need or curiosity.

Throughout, the book requires several balancing acts. Its aims are doggedly practical, but to be practical it must be theoretical. Moreover, to be practical, it must be specific, and the specifics must be drawn from my own teaching and from the teaching I have observed. I must be personal, anecdotal at times; I must also generalize my particulars, stress their broader applications, without rendering them vacuously abstract. I must also do a balancing act in tone. I write to perplexed teachers out of my own perplexities, but I will be offering my own scenarios and experiments as guides, saying, "Here is how it might be done." My aim, however, is neither self-indulgent reminiscence nor dogmatic prescription. I do have theories, but no theoretical axe to grind. My method, as in most classrooms, is to set and explain the agenda, and to provoke and assist others to think through their own options and priorities. My tentative, conversational style will, I hope, seem suitable.

This book could not have been written at all had I not had the joy and the privilege of spending the past seventeen years among colleagues the most resourceful, dedicated, and versatile I have ever known, at a young public university restless and creative in its commitment to teaching and learning. The book is dedicated to them, with special thanks to James Broderick, creator of our Center for Teaching. It is dedicated as well to over three thousand students who have slowly taught me whatever I know about learning and teaching.

BEYOND THE BOOKS

ONE

Styles and Rhythms
of Learning and Teaching

I

The only practical way to think about teaching is
to think first about learning and then about teaching as an ancil-
lary activity, a cause of learning, a process of interaction whose
goal is to further knowledge and understanding. Different styles
or modes of teaching fit different styles and stages of learning and
intellectual development. Effective teaching begins with a sense
of decorum, and the resourceful teacher possesses a working repertoire of styles and knows when and how to use them. In this
preparatory chapter, we will recall some familiar styles or models
of learning and teaching, and some ideas about curricular design,
and will suggest some meaningful correlations among them. We
need this theoretical context for what will follow.

Israel Scheffler's three "philosophical models of teaching"—
actually models of learning—are a useful point of departure.
Scheffler's *impression* model assumes that knowledge is impressed from without on the student's mind. Learning is a process of acquisition, accumulation, and generalization from what is
accumulated. His *insight* model assumes that knowledge pre-
exists in some form, and that teaching is educing or drawing it
out, bringing to articulation. Students learn by coming to know
their knowledge, to understand their insights. His *rule* model assumes that learning is a process of refining the rules or principles
by which we know or understand. To learn is to grow in ration-

1

ality, in the capacity for reasoned deliberation. Scheffler believes that these three models incorporate the many approaches to teaching and learning found throughout the history of educational theory.

Not surprisingly, he also believes that each model in isolation is flawed and incomplete. Corrected in and through synthesis, they provide a single, complex model. Learning and teaching necessarily include impression, insight, and rule. I am not equipped to judge his model in the abstract, nor is this the place to try. I am interested in how we can use it. What can we learn when we take it to be a plausible hypothesis and relate it to a number of other concepts of teaching modes and styles? (We will have some trouble keeping these two terms from blurring, so let's examine both in some detail.)

We can easily discover certain common patterns and biases. Jerome Bruner speaks of an *expository* and a *hypothetical* mode of teaching. Paulo Freire distinguishes a *banking* model from a *dialogic* model. David Riesman observes a *didactic* style and an *evocative* style. All three are trying to typify antithetical kinds of interaction between teacher and student; their antitheses have much in common. In the denigrative first term of each pair—expository, banking, didactic—it is assumed that the teacher is active, the student passive; the teacher gives, the student receives; the teacher directs, the student performs under direction. In the commendatory second terms—hypothetical, dialogic, evocative—it is assumed that teacher and student are active collaborators. Each brings experience, knowledge, and insight to the enterprise. The teacher guides and provokes the student to clearer and fuller insight and to autonomous (or self-directed) discovery. The first terms reflect Scheffler's impression model; the second, his insight model. Their very language commits them to it. With the help of Scheffler's critique, we could see the falseness of the antitheses, if such were our purpose, and we will confront the falseness later in practical contexts.

But what happens in these dualistic models to Scheffler's third or *rule* model? The idea of teaching and learning as the cultivation of rules or principles for knowing, inquiring, understanding? Is it left somewhere outside or somewhere in between? The question is not merely theoretical. We need to answer it if only because, at present, the most prestigious views of teaching and learning center our obligations as teachers in this rule model. We must teach students "how to think," how to conceptualize. We need, says Scheffler, "to introduce students" to "principled deliberation." They need to learn the principles or rules that we ourselves acknowledge as "fundamental, general, and impartial in the various departments of thought and action" (129–33).

Suppose we agree. Does this teaching assume the impression model or the insight model? Is this cultivation of the powers of reasoned deliberation to be impressed on the student's mind, or is it there already as "insight" to be drawn out? Can the rules of inquiry and assessment be taught? Scheffler's own language assumes so: we "introduce students" to "principles"; we "teach rationality" to "interiorize these principles." Or can they be learned only through evocation, dialogue, shared hypothesizing? The Platonist believes that rationality can be educed, while the Aristotelian seeks to impress it.

The problem is difficult but inescapable, with fundamental pedagogical consequences. Notice how it operates in Frank Smith's psycholinguistic account of comprehension and learning. Smith believes that all learning must begin with the "theory of the world" already in the student's head. This "theory" is a model of reality arranged in interconnected categories. It is "implicit" but "there"; presumably it is the source of what Scheffler calls insight. But wait. Smith says this theory in the head includes "discourse structures" and "genre schemes." These are the conventional patterns of intention and expectation without which we could not understand anything we read. But how do these conventional patterns get into the head? Presumably they are not innate, but must be learned. Presumably they are among the rules or principles of what Scheffler calls rationality. Can they be evoked, hypothesized by the student, or must they first be impressed, expounded, and demonstrated by the teacher?

In almost every course at every level, I remake the same unnerving discovery. I ask a student to give "reasons" for a judgment or an inference, and when the student gives something else, I ask, "Is that a reason?" only to find that many students are not sure what a reason is. What then am I to do but expound didactically what a reason is? And then when I ask, "Do you see what I mean?" do I not mean, "Do you get it? Has it become a part of your 'theory in the head'? Has what I impressed become part of your insight?"

I seem to be reverting to Paulo Freire's "banking model" (which Freire himself rejects), in which the teacher "deposits" knowledge and understanding in the student's mind. Can Freire himself avoid it? For him, teaching and learning begin when students and teacher get together an agenda of problems and perceptions. They then organize this agenda into a structure of dialectical relationships, moving as they do so from abstract to concrete back to abstract, from whole to part and back to whole. But what if the student cannot yet recognize what is abstract and what is concrete, what is part and what is whole? Can such a recognition be evoked out of student insight, or must it initially be defined, explained by the teacher? Surely Freire is right that "I cannot think *for others* or *without others,* nor can others think *for me.* Even if the people's thinking is superstitious or naive, it is only as they rethink their assumptions in action that they can change" (100). But how will they learn to identify assumptions, to carry on that "rethinking" process? Jane Martin seems to say what Freire says, but notice her qualifiers and the temporal order of learning she implies:

> Seeing is something each person has to do for himself. No one can do your seeing for you. Others can point out things to you, give you relevant information, *enlarge your conceptual repertoire, and all the rest,* but in the last analysis [does she not mean "the last stage"?] you have to come through and do the actual job—the seeing—yourself. (emphasis added, 164)

Presumably the actual job of seeing is done with and through that "enlarged conceptual repertoire" provided by "others."

At different stages or contexts of learning, these opposites—

call them what we will, expository and hypothetical, didactic and evocative, banking and dialogic—are needed, and needed in rhythmic alternation. Impression and insight interact dialectically—that is, each generates and regenerates the other. And the learning of rules of rational deliberation belongs to both: they must be impressed, expounded; they must be "seen" or discovered. Discovery and invention—finding and creating—are aspects of the same process. Without insight, what value is there in all the teacher impresses? Without impression, how can student insight clarify and grow? Without rules of rationality, how can they develop together into systematic understanding? The different styles or modes must be combined and coordinated. The issue is utilitarian: what coordinations of style or mode, in what order, best serve the ends of learning in a particular context: to know more, to know with livelier insight, to know more rationally?

II

The answer is, "It depends." It depends on the point in the structure of the course, and on the stage in the process of learning. What do we mean anyway when we refer to a course's "structure"? The Structuralist philosophy of the past generation could provide us with theoretical definitions, but we need not get that theoretical. The educational theorists I am drawing on also imply different meanings of "structure." Alas, the most important is also the most difficult to understand; it is also the most fundamental and therefore needs to be understood first. My difficulty here in constructing my own exposition is precisely what it addresses.

Paul Hirst reminds us that every subject matter has its own intrinsic structure, its logic of interconnected concepts, its disciplines of method. But this structure is not necessarily the same as the structure or order of learning the subject matter. The sequence of steps taken to solve a geometry problem is not the same as the order of steps set out to prove the solution. Or as Hirst says, the question of how to teach history is not a historical question; one is a matter of logical arrangement, the other of temporal order. The composition teacher well knows how hard and how important it is for the student writer to learn that the composing process differs in structure from the composed product. If this book of mine has logical structure, that structure has little resemblance to the order in which I have learned how to write it and the order in which the actual writing was done. The order in which a student learns is not the order in which what is learned is structured in her mind.

And yet, the two obviously have to be related. Some modern linguists might say that one is a "transformation" of the other. The order of teaching must be based, says Hirst, on an understanding of the logical structure of the subject; one cannot design the first without the second. I cannot figure out at what point in my exposition to include Hirst's ideas without understanding how those ideas relate logically to the rest.

These heady concepts should become clearer in later chapters. The real principles of course design remain a mystery for many of us. Our planning normally stops with: (1) what will I include? and (2) how much? The real principles involve the coordination of three variables: (1) the logical structure of the subject matter; (2) the order in which the subject matter can best be learned; and (3) the stage of intellectual development of the learners. What element *needs* to be learned first? What element *can* be learned first? If the two answers are the same, we are in luck. If not, we have to make compromises.

For now, let's turn to another, simpler model of the process of learning. Alfred North Whitehead suggests that we think of learning as a rhythm of three stages (with numerous eddies). The rhythm begins and ends with freedom; the middle is discipline. The first stage, *romance,* is a prediscipline awakening to the novelty and possibilities of a subject, an arousing of interest and curiosity. The second stage, *precision,* is a disciplined attention to intrinsic elements—fact, methods, concepts. The third stage, *generalization,* expands into syntheses and applications, extrinsic connections. Stage One: hypothetical exploration; Stage Two: analysis and validation; Stage Three: implication, extrapolation.

Of course, Whitehead is speaking of a rhythm that runs through several years. Can it also apply to a single college course? I believe it can, and in later chapters I will be testing this belief.

The implications of such a rhythmic pattern for the shape and pedagogy of a single course are these. The *first segment* or (roughly) month is predisciplinary, exploratory; its materials, assignments, and teaching styles are selected as most immediately provocative or suggestive. The teacher serves chiefly as provocateur, evocator. Students are expected and encouraged to venture, to hypothesize, to "see the possibilities." The *second segment* or month is the time for precision, for the work most difficult, most demanding of discipline, methodical study. Materials, assignments, styles are chosen accordingly, and in student performance a premium is placed on acquisition, technique, discipline. In the *third segment* or month broader connections and applications are emphasized; students are guided toward rational synthesis; materials, assignments, and teaching modes are chosen to this end. I know that course materials do not break down so neatly, that teaching styles overlap, but shifts of emphasis are possible and appropriate.

I also know that the reality of any class population challenges any such neat scheme. The three "stages" also designate different individual styles of learning and different stages of intellectual development. Different students respond differently to these three pedagogies; some resist one, some another. Take, for example, my own recent class in nineteenth-century English fiction. Suppose we begin with an unstructured, free-wheeling discussion of first impressions of *Bleak House* based on its beginnings. I welcome, entertain, and engage with a whole miscellany—some would say "mess"—of perceptions, reactions, and associations. There is no sharp focus, no disciplined testing. Some students love it; in fact, they love little else. Others, already highly disciplined, ready (they suppose) for analysis and validation, are uneasy or even angered with such goings on. No tolerance for "romance." I try to assure them that our romance has two legitimate ends: (1) this is the only empirical way of finding out possible responses to the book's beginnings; (2) this is the most legitimate way of forming an agenda of questions for the more precise analytic talks to follow. Perhaps they will trust me.

Then, we pass to that second stage. We will now, say, do a quiz on the main episodes that plot the novel. On the basis of this quiz, we will conceptualize the kinds of events and interpret the logics of their interconnections. Why do things happen as they do? What does this structure mean? In the face of such precision, my "romance" students may well be turned off or tuned out by the lowering of temperature and the raising of logical intensity. Somehow I must show them that, without this precision, their first impressions and responses cannot grow and reveal.

Likewise, when we move on to the third stage and see the novel in contexts—generic, historical, authorial—other students will complain that Teacher should have "told" them these things first so that they would "know how to read the novel." These are the folks who want premature generalization, who feel it legitimate only to read a text in and by the conceptual structure of a course, and thus to prepare themselves to perform on papers and exams. Meanwhile, our "romance" explorers may well feel scornful of such generalizations, and our "precision" disciplinarians may distrust them. My job is to persuade all of a need for stylistic tolerance of each other, to persuade them that all three stages are essential. It's never easy, but the rhythm remains a good guide, and the teaching repertoire is eventually appreciated.

So let's look more closely at how the repertoire can be adapted to the rhythm. Scheffler's three models of teaching make no reference, of course, to the process structure of Whitehead. But we can arrange them in the same sequence. Scheffler's insight model suggests a pedagogy of educing, of provoking, and this suits Whitehead's first stage. (It also suits Freire's first or "generative" stage.) Scheffler's impression model suggests the process of imparting new information, demonstrating and instructing new concepts and methods. Such a process suits Whitehead's "precision" stage with its rigors. Scheffler's rule model in its emphases and goals suggests Whitehead's "generalization" stage. For here, we focus on principles that are "fundamental, general and impartial, in the various departments of thought and action." Here the student proceeds toward "principled deliberation" and "the building of autonomous and rational character" (131). He now has acquired (we hope) the "conceptual repertoire" with which to make applications more on his own. Allowing for necessary overlaps, and for Whitehead's "eddies" back and forth, we can see that at different stages in a course, different modes of learning and teaching are fitting.

We can understand the rhythm, too, in terms of changing student-teacher interactions. The process of learning in a course is an alternation (dialectic, if you like) of community and autonomy. The student enters alone, joins a collaborative community of learners, and emerges (if the course succeeds) with a fuller, truer autonomy . . . the community remembered, internalized. At times, the emphasis is on group dialogue, cooperation, consensus building. I would stress this at the start of any course or course unit, to build or renew a sense of community and trust, to generate together a shared thematics, a sharing of provocative insights—hence, Whitehead's "romance." At other times the student is closely focused on interchange (spoken or silent) with the teacher, is being "impressed" or instructed. The teacher's style is necessarily didactic and expository. This is the stage for precision. And at still other times, the student is necessarily "tuned out." He has been stimulated or provoked through the romance, the sharing of insights and possibilities. He has been instructed in new information, concepts, methods. He now thinks more autonomously, pursues his own directions in material and issue. What complicates classroom interaction is that it may well include all three at once (different students at different stages in the rhythm). While this situation cannot be planned, it can be planned for. Some classes will be lively communal exchanges, some will be sustained discourse (instruction) from the teacher, and some will be quieter, more thoughtful or "private" workshop sessions. Teacher and student alike should expect and accept this alternation as normal and necessary.

Another way of understanding our idea of a course rhythm is suggested by Jerome Bruner's essay on discovery in *On Know-*

ing. Bruner is arguing for teaching styles that encourage "discovery," and who could disagree? Bruner asserts that discovery is encouraged by the teaching style he calls hypothetical—that is, by teaching that involves the student actively in directing the processes of learning. It is all too easy either to endorse or to reject such an idea outright, but first we should understand it. And we cannot understand it if we speak of discovery as a single enterprise. What kind of discovery, what object of discovery, do we have in mind?

Whitehead's rhythm suggests different kinds at different stages. In the first stage, we look for the discovery of issues and possibilities generated largely from what is already known. In the second, we want the discovery of more—and more precise—knowledge, concepts, and internal patterns. In the third, we promote the discovery of general contexts, external implications. Different processes are involved in discovering a possibility or hypothesis, discovering a relevant fact or applicable concept, discovering a thematic or extrinsic relationship. Internal and external connections are not discovered the same way.

In using "internal" and "external," I am borrowing a distinction made by Jane Martin in her discussion of understanding as seeing connections. The distinction can be adapted to our Whitehead rhythm. To teach an understanding of a subject, we guide students to see its connections, some external, some internal. But there are two kinds of external connection that concern us. In our initial stage, we explore external connections that bring together new problems and possibilities with the student's previous knowledge, insight, Smith's "theory of the world" already in his head. At the end, we pursue external connections that bring together what the student has learned with more general principles and implications. In the middle, we emphasize internal connections, interconnections of information, idea, technique. First, how do we respond initially to *Bleak House*? Second, how is *Bleak House* "put together" so as to amplify and refine those responses? Third, how does *Bleak House* connect with our growing contexts? Such is the rhythm. And our goal, however far off, is that our students become readers for whom reading a novel is at once romantic, precise, and broadly synthetic.

Like any abstract model, this rhythm of ours appears overly simple and schematic, and we must not confuse it with the real calendar of a specific course. It is meant only as a guide. If nothing else, it can lead us to a new perspective on diversity in teaching styles and modes. Many of us begin (as I began) with a simple absolutism, one that still haunts a public awareness of education even as it invalidates much personnel review of teaching: there is Good teaching and Bad; there are Good teachers and Bad. The realization that it is not so simple leads, as it leads students, to an exhilarating but extreme relativism. There are as many styles of teaching as there are teachers; each of us teaches in his own way, and who can say any one of them is better? This is the intellectual stage that some developmentalists call *multiplicity*. From such a helpless and deterministic pluralism, we may now move to a third stage. The "good" or "bad" of teaching must be measured according to the kinds of teaching called for within the changing contexts of a course. This is a more rational and useful position. William Perry calls it *contextual relativism*, and Barbara Clinchy and Claire Zimmerman revise his term to *contextualism*. But Perry and Clinchy and Zimmerman are not speaking of curricular contexts: they are speaking of the broader contexts of learning within which all courses must be understood.

III

As they do, they broaden our own attention. I have just tried to construct a way of understanding the internal connections of our subject, styles or modes of teaching and designs of course and course units. What happens to this construction when we place it in a larger context? How is it connected to the larger rhythms of intellectual development in students?

William Perry gives us yet another model of triadic progression, the model applied above. The first stage is a simple dualism of attitude toward truth, correctness of fact, method, definition, and intellectual authority. It is absolutist. The second stage, multiplicity, is the discovery that truth, correctness, authority are not absolutes, and a resultant belief that they are "all matters of opinion," of individual style, preference, point of view. The third, contextualism, transcends the second, in the belief that truth, correctness, authority can be understood rationally but only as relative to context. Opinion is not merely an individual accident; point of view is (or can be) a rationally comprehensible perspective. (My ultimate test of a student's intellectual development is whether the student understands the nature of intellectual perspective; this is the hardest thing we teach in any discipline and possibly the most important.)

Certainly a significant number of our students come to us expecting a kind and a degree of intellectual authority that many of us consider illusory. Even some older students have a similar expectation of order and discipline, not necessarily because they are at an "absolutist" stage, but because life experiences and copings have made or kept them authoritarians. Such students enter a college course with the dualistic attitude that there are right and wrong answers. If we begin the course with a "romance" stage—predisciplinary insight, untested feasibility, puzzlement—they will find such a stage chaotic, unsettling, or frustrating. To provide at the start the precision they demand would be premature. We can only reassure them that the stage of precision will come when we are ready for it.

If we adopt the developmental model, then certain pedagogical questions arise. To what extent can we guide or motivate the development? To what extent should we? How can we begin the course by provoking the dualistic student to discover multiplicity, to realize that uncertainty, possibility, diversity of insight are legitimate—more than that, necessary, creative, even enjoyable? For this is what we must do if our curricular rhythm is to begin in romance.

Clinchy and Zimmerman imply that to do this we must show students that their opinions and insights matter—even when they are merely opinions or what Clinchy and Zimmerman call "ready made reactions." We must, as Freire argues, begin with such opinions (even what he calls superstitions) in order to compose our agenda, and then proceed to decode them. We must begin by bringing out the "theories of the world" already in the students' heads—for this is where the students begin. What, we ask, do these opinions really mean? Why do people hold them? How do they differ from and resemble the opinions of others?

I recall a good example from teaching an introductory interdisciplinary course called Law and Justice. We began with a documentary film about everyday police behavior. The film provoked a lively and prejudicial, even superstitious, debate. Some students assured us from experience that most policemen spend most of their time beating up teenage pot smokers. Others angrily defended policemen as blue knights protecting neighborhoods against psychotic hoodlums. Shortly we would introduce our students to disciplined studies of actual police behavior and motivation. But not yet. First we needed that undisciplined exchange of impressions, prejudices, myths; and we needed to help students become actively aware of them, to decode them, to begin to see how they were formed, and to generate an agenda of issues. Another example. Recently I began a graduate seminar in the teaching of literature with this assignment: each member was asked to present an argument in behalf of one literary text that should be taught. The results generated the same undisciplined exchange of prejudices and myths, and out of our composing and decoding of these we formed our agenda. Similar beginnings in romance are observed in various fields. I observed a teacher open an introductory psychology course by asking the class, "What do you think science is?" I observed an anthropologist begin a course by assigning a reading and then simply asking each student in turn what the student thought he or she had learned from it. To begin any such course or study with, "First we must establish certain authoritative definitions," or "First we must learn how to perform certain technical operations," is to miss the point and to short-circuit the developmental process.

One result of "romance" openings is, for some students, a radical shift in their image of what a teacher should be. Many exhilarated lower-division students evaluate their teachers and courses exclusively in terms of the teacher's tolerance, openness, and willingness to allow anyone to state his or her "ideas." This is the romance of multiplicity. But eventually it brings the unnerving discovery that Clinchy and Zimmerman describe. Students feel liberated, but some of them also begin to feel oppressed by the sense that they do not know what to do with the freedom, how to get beyond mere multiplicity, how to choose rationally among alternative opinions and to make reasoned decisions. This is the discovery of "cognitive incompetence," the feeling that one is free to think and expected to think but does not know how. Robert Frost long ago observed that teachers are forever ordering students to think but seldom showing them how to do it. The pedagogical response to this unnerving discovery—but not before students make it—is to lead the way from romance to precision.

In leading the way to precision, the teacher necessarily adopts a different role, a more didactic and expository mode. She provides or locates relevant information and enlarges conceptual repertoires. She shows students how to think, how to acquire knowledge, examine and test it, organize it. Some students will necessarily resist this shift. They will see the teacher as having lost her tolerance, having reasserted her true absolutism about right and wrong, and having simply imposed her own style. The more pragmatic or cynical ones will try to imitate the teacher's intellectual style or mode simply because she is "in charge" and will judge them according to "what she wants." The more sensitive ones may experience the feeling Clinchy and Zimmerman also describe well. Having gained voices (or perspectives) of their own, they may feel that they are now losing them, being robbed of them, and beginning to speak in teachers' voices or in voices that simply react to teachers. Clinchy and Zimmerman associate this phenomenon with sophomore slump. I am much less sanguine about the pace. I find bright juniors and seniors—indeed, even some Ph.D. students—struggling still to find or keep their own voices. Some remain anxious about multiplicity, are willing to move on only when they can jump from an earlier stage of certainty to a later one. Others will persist in a distrust of teachers' intellectual authority which, carried to an extreme, prevents their learning.

The difficulties are inevitable. Every new course taken seems to reenact the process, to force students once more into a confusing multiplicity, to show them again their cognitive incompetence. This is another reason why the individual course rhythm is so important. Each course needs its own sense of closure, of synthesis and assimilation, so that the student finishes each course with some feeling of personal control or autonomy, however partial, temporary, or even illusory. And to accomplish this, we must somehow move to our third stage, move from multiplicity through precision to a final stage of contextual reasoning and generalization. How these crucial pedagogical moves can be negotiated will be part of our inquiry in later chapters.

But first we must make our own move from theories and models to the dynamic, often nagging, realities of a classroom— any classroom. When Robert Scholes makes this move, he says, "Time now to tackle smaller fry and let our world shrink to the compass of the classroom once again" (129). Knowing him as a teacher, I'm positive his metaphors are tongue-in-cheek. Here if anywhere is where our models have to live. And when I say "our," I refer to teachers in most fields. It is well to remind ourselves that our pedagogical problems and options are very interdisciplinary.

TWO

The Class as Text and Performance

      With the above models in mind, we are better prepared to observe what actually happens in a classroom. We have acquired a number of conceptual distinctions that may be useful in distinguishing the styles and modes that teachers use: *impression* versus *insight; expository* versus *hypothetical; banking* versus *dialogic; didactic* versus *evocative;* even the old familiar "lecture" versus "discussion." But they will be useful only insofar as we employ them as imperfect guides, not as masterful blinders. Every class session is a unique text, and as we learn to read it as we do any other complex text, every generic term takes on various meanings and enters into changing interrelations. Every teaching has features of performance; but to read the performance, we must keep in mind the individuality of the performer and the particulars of the curricular scene.

      Let's begin with some concrete examples, half a dozen brief readings of teachers at work. Although they represent actual observations, the names and personalities have been changed to protect confidentiality. Besides, class observation is a confidential business. Here is our cast of characters. "Thomas" is teaching major British writers. "Rosen" is introducing psychology, and "Schmidt" is completing an introduction to western intellectual history. "Stone" is teaching urban history, and "Reilly" is introducing modern political ideas. Finally, "Russo's" chief concern is with sociological method. What can we observe about their styles or modes?

I

To listen to Thomas teach, one would suppose that he is merely drawing out student impressions of what is most "strange" in Chaucer's world. He is being what is called evocative. He asks for a formulation of this thematic world largely in terms of student insights. He provides no information; some students volunteer it unasked, saying what they "know" about the Middle Ages, whereupon he acts skeptical and directs attention back to the text. He calls frequently for examples not as proof but by way of specification. He resists judgments—of Chaucer, of students—but welcomes all insights, conflates and synthesizes them, and returns them for further dialogue.

The class had been primed the day before with study questions, and these questions sound like an interrogative reframing of a lecture Thomas decided not to give. They articulate his own theme, and this theme is being established through a controlled teacher-student interaction, so that students may well think they are discovering it themselves. Thomas's mode is actually a concealed exposition, while his classroom style is hypothetical—that is, students help to control the agenda. He is far more didactic than he seems.

Rosen, teaching Introduction to Psychology, is also evocative. He is evoking a "way of looking at the world" that was Freudianism, as Thomas was doing with Chaucer's world. But Rosen calls for other mental operations. His key commands, repeated with a warm enthusiasm that belies their imperative nature, are "Imagine! Imagine! the powerful impact, the tremendous impact! You see? You see?" He gives little information (it is in the assigned text). Instead, he tries to realize—to feel and imagine—this intellectual world for the students. Complexities are finessed; critical assessments are postponed. The style is dramatic; the teacher is a medium, a magician, for whom key words carry power and insight.

He asks many questions, but they are directed exclusively at drawing out the implications of key words, not (as with Thomas) at evoking student insights. The questions are repeated, redirected; he seems eager to project his own sense of meaning into students' minds. "When you see a word like this, you ask yourself what other word could have been used and wasn't used, and why." YOU YOU YOU. Yet it is evident that what he wants YOU to "see" and say is what HE is getting at. And what he is getting at, he often implies, should be obvious, and he won't expound it. When an unrelated response is offered, he says "there is a point to it" (not pausing to explain the point), but "it is not what I am driving at." When they guess what he is driving at, he shares with them an infectious delight in recognition. The mode is at once powerfully evocative and strongly didactic.

While Rosen tries to project his own mental exuberance into the student's mind, Schmidt (teaching modern intellectual history) seems to possess extraordinary insight into what students are thinking. And while Thomas reached doggedly for such insight through a probing of the words students used, Schmidt needs scarcely more than a hint. (It is noteworthy that Thomas was teaching his course for the first time, while Schmidt has taught hers annually for many years.) Schmidt is conducting a late session of synthesizing review, "making a diagram of the course," trying to "do this *with you*." Whereas Rosen often asked, "You see? You see?" and Thomas, "What is your impression? How does it connect?" Schmidt says, "You know! You know!" and urges students to know their knowledge in terms of the diagram being constructed. The enterprise is communal; she often breaks in with, "Others, help!" When they draw a blank, she urges gently, "Come on. You can think of *something. . . .* That's it!" Almost anything can be a beginning, the start of a thread of retrieval and connection. Follow-up questions take many analytical forms: What? Who? How so? What do you mean by that? Excuse for what? Can you draw that out a little more?

Words have as much force here as for Thomas and Rosen, but for Schmidt they must come *after* understanding, for they "encapsulate what we've been talking about." A new word comes up, and Schmidt says, "I would make you work out what it meant if we hadn't worked out what it meant before we came to the word." (Note the authority of "would make you" together with the cooperative "we" of working out.) Schmidt often seems to anticipate what will be said: "Are you thinking that . . . ? Yes? Tell us about it." On some occasions, the saying is not what she is "looking for," but she welcomes it and pauses to explore its relevance; but always it is clear that she knows and that they know she knows what she is after. Occasionally she intercedes to explain a connection, but otherwise the style or mode is not expository. It is less evocative than Rosen's but equally didactic. The "banking" has been done earlier in the course, and now the student is to pay back with interest and insight.

By contrast, Stone and Reilly come close to the traditional "lecture" format, but the designation is superficial, and they differ from each other as much as from Rosen and Schmidt. For one thing, Stone's presentation (of Boston social history) is chiefly informative. Reilly's (an introduction to political ideas) is chiefly interpretive: she is expounding ideas as outlooks, as attitudes, and distinguishing some that are easily confused. For another thing, Stone's rhetorical mode is argument: he offers his ample information in support of a position, and while students are not invited openly to debate or dispute it, some obviously feel eager to do so. Reilly's mode is reflective: the meaning of a position, not its validity, is at issue here (and Reilly is dealing with very controversial positions). Stone is more personal in intellectual stance while less personal in style. His style is public: he is the public elder who suggests, "My advice to you is . . ." Reilly's style, quite impersonal, is private: quiet, meditative, searching, it imparts the hypnotic quality of an interior monologue. Yet it is a monologue into which students evidently feel ready and willing to join, as if an extraordinary attentiveness had included their minds in its process. Thus one "lecture" is a public report-demonstration, while the other "lecture" is an intimate conversation with the self.

Finally, Russo's manner (he is teaching sociology of law) is as much that of the "public lecture" as Stone's, yet its structure is dialogic. He calls frequently for student "input," and, like Thomas, he has primed the class for it. They have been given an assignment. They are expected to come to class with knowledge of the text and with their critical notes. His questioning is as ana-

lytic and sequential as Schmidt's, though the questions are modeled more on scientific method (he is a social scientist; Schmidt is
a historian): What were the indications? What were the disadvan-
tages and advantages of such a procedure? What does the evidence suggest? What conclusions were drawn and how? The dialogue takes the shape of a critical process, at once structured and
lively.

Is this lecture or discussion? The distinction has little meaning. Is it didactic or evocative? It is both. The teacher is demonstrating a method; he is also evoking an awareness of how a theory was intended, tested, and found flawed. How well has he
succeeded? Is that what he should have been trying to do? What
about Thomas, Rosen, Schmidt, Stone, and Reilly? Obviously we
are not ready to judge. The generic terms help us observe what is
going on, but their reliability is unstable. The observable styles
are various and versatile, but they are only one aspect of what
goes on in a classroom.

II

A class session is a sociolinguistic event, a cultural organism in action. Here are Seven Ways of Looking at the
Event. They may not be exhaustive, and certainly I did not discover them, but they are all important, and to some degree con-
trollable, and our teaching is impoverished if we ignore them.

A class has its *ecology*, and the ecology matters, however
little we can control it: time of day, size and shape of room, air (or
lack of it), light (or dark), surrounding noise, furnishings, apparatus, and clutter. It matters how the people of the event use or
misuse this environment, their spaces, accesses, distances, movements. How many teachers have thought, "If I had a different
classroom, I could teach this class better?" How many have
shared my troubled sense of the anonymity and transiency of
"my" classroom (fit emblem of the brevity and discontinuity of
my encounters with these students)? The room is "mine" and
"ours" only during the assigned fifty or eighty minutes. We wait
for another class to vacate, leaving behind not just their enig-

matic blackboards and empty cups, their forgotten notebooks and curious handouts, but also the aura of the otherness of their learning and teaching. It is fascinating to watch how one of us enters this foreign place and performs the ceremonial gestures of temporary possession and community. All of this has its impact on learning.

Every session has its *logics* as well, its intellectual structures and sequences, its texture of governing ideas, its proportions and transitions. Sometimes the teacher is conscious of them, sometimes even the student, sometimes neither. Some teachers regularly signal to students what these are; others (ill-advisedly, I think) take them for granted. Teaching is, among other things, a composing process. How much and how manifestly structured a good class must be is an open question.

Whatever they are, the logics can be communicated only in language. Certain prevailing kinds and levels of language are used by teacher and students; sometimes they are quite similar, sometimes quite different, even separate or divisive. For the students, every class is a process of learning the teacher's language, and every teacher willy-nilly is a language instructor. Many teachers are unaware of the languages they use: the relative degrees of technicality and formality, the key syntactic forms, the terms and tones. Revealing phrases echo through a class: "you will remember that" (?), "our next step is," "that isn't what I'm looking for," "on the other hand," "by the way," "this is important." Sometimes questions are asked. What kinds are habitually asked? What kinds of answers are habitually given? Do the answerers understand the kinds of questions? What kinds of "wrong" or "irrelevant" responses are heard? Is there, as Mina Shaughnessy would ask, a logic in the errors?

Every session has its *rhetoric*. Certain forms and methods are used to achieve certain ends: informative, explanatory, persuasive. Know it or not, the teacher is seeking to persuade the student of the significance of what is being communicated or the necessity of doing what is required. The teacher uses texts, exercises, demonstrations, examples, analogies, motivational appeals. What kinds? Why these?

Logics, languages, and rhetorics do not emerge in a human vacuum. Every session has its *dramaturgy* and its *sociology* (my humanist biases tell me they are closely related). Members of the class play interactive roles. We can detect clues in pacing, voicing, nonverbal gesture, degrees of intensity and involvement. How does the teacher use authority (or power) and what kinds? The class has its *politics*, its directions and commands, invitations, rewards and threats. Teachers are often startled to learn how they appear to behave. Some are perplexed by the issues of pedagogical authority and need help in learning how to present themselves in ways they consider legitimate. The dramaturgy matters.

Every session has its *contexts*, some in the mind of the teacher, others in the mind of the student—and often the twain do not meet. The class has its relations to larger designs, other courses and disciplines, academic goals and values, extramural preoccupations and influences. No class is an island. What uses are made of such foreign relations? What use *should* be made is a legitimate issue of strategy and priority.

Finally, every session has its *effects*, cognitive and otherwise. The outcomes are what matter. What manifestations can be noted, and is the teacher aware of them? Most teachers have ended a class with the frustrated sense that "things went well. I did all I could. Students seemed attentive, interested, responsive. Nevertheless, I have only the roughest of hunches of how much and how well they learned what I wanted them to learn." There is no simple remedy. It is impossible to instruct and evaluate equally at the same time. But many teachers limit their efforts to the periodic, "Does everyone understand?" or "Are there any questions?"—efforts that normally produce few useful discoveries. How many students can identify themselves as the nonunderstanders, and how many nonunderstanders have a clue as to what kinds of questions to ask?

III

Nothing that happens in a classroom is more essential than the processes of formulating questions and pursuing answers. "For us," Nancy Hoffman writes, "the question/answer process is the nexus between teaching and learning. This is the way we indicate what we think is important or difficult or particularly intriguing; this is the way we get clues to what is going on in the minds of our students" (62). And yet, for many teachers the process comes down to three anxieties: (1) how to ask questions that will evoke a quick and lively discussion; (2) how to respond to answers that seem wrong, vague, or irrelevant; and (3) how to handle questions that seem trivial, irrelevant (at the moment), or (for the moment) unanswerable by the teacher. The anxieties are legitimate, but there are many more considerations.

The point of departure has to be: Why ask questions at all? What do we want them to do? The answer "to evoke a lively discussion" is hardly enough. If questioning does not promote learning and does not help us measure learning, it is useless. Second, what different kinds of questions are there? Only if we know can we then judge which kind(s) will best serve our purposes at a given moment in the course. In his fine essay "Questioning," Thomas Kasulis identifies three kinds: questions of content, questions of class process, and questions of persons in the class. The scheme doesn't go far enough. Third, how do we correlate the kinds of questions we ask with the kinds of student performance we will expect and evaluate. If the questions we test by differ in kind and emphasis from the questions we have stressed in class, how can we expect a positive outcome? Fourth, in what sequence should kinds of questions be arranged? The answer is double: questions must follow some logic of inquiry; questions must also follow an order in which students can learn.

Hoffman emphasizes another dimension of questioning. Questions call for distinct kinds of mental operation in every discipline: summarizing, comparing, analyzing, interpreting (stating a meaning), evaluating, explaining (accounting for), defining, and so on. Do the students really understand what kind of mental operation a question calls for, and how to perform that operation? Are the questions grounded in a common operational vocabulary of the class? Knowing how to formulate questions requires knowing what kinds of questions are possible and what kinds of mental performances they call for. If we want students to learn to ask good questions, we will have to teach them these ideas, these conceptual forms.

If they have not learned them, or if our questions are uncoordinated or out of sequence, then we can expect answers that are erroneous, vague, or irrelevant. What do we do about such answers? First we seek out causes in the way we are questioning. Second we seek out causes in the ways students are learning (or not learning). Most of us, alas, can recall our own variations of Hoffman's example:

> Professor: Would someone please explain dual labor market theory?
>
> Carol: Well, it's because women are always low paid . . .
>
> Professor: Hmmmm . . . Joe, you try.
>
> Joe: Well, in the nineteenth century, the country started to industrialize and . . .
>
> Professor: Let me stop you there, OK? That's history. Dual market theory postulates . . . (62)

Did Carol and Joe not know the answer? Or rather, did they not know how to answer the question? Either or both may be true. If our priority is student learning, we had better find out. We can try during (as part of) class discussion, if this seems useful, or we can design instruments (writings, exercises) for outside use, if not.

Our perspective must shift from how we teach to how students learn. We stop confronting students' learning problems merely by correcting errors or prescribing tactics, and begin exploring with students how they are learning and why not more or better. The established impulse is to welcome what seems right or relevant and to correct what is wrong, reject what seems irrelevant. We are afraid to get "off the point" or to give "false signals." In fact, the established impulse often fails. The signal it gives is that a student should not commit herself unless she is certain she is correct or relevant. She will learn to say simply, "I don't know." We want students to take risks, learn from errors, but our signals say the opposite. In fact, "errors" and "irrelevancies" may have their own logic, as Mina Shaughnessy taught us. A "wrong" answer or an "off the wall" comment or question may reveal lots, open up problems, offer a new angle. The most productive response to a wrong answer is not, "The correct answer is . . ." but, "How did you arrive at that answer? Let's figure out the source of the mistake." The most productive response to an irrelevant comment is not, "That's not what I'm looking for," but, "Could you explain to us how that is related, or why we need it at this point?"

Occasionally, we discover with dismay whole patterns of irrelevancy. Students habitually ask and tell us kinds of things that differ basically from what we want them to ask and tell. I recall observing a course in sociological theory whose students, neophyte social workers, wanted instead a practical grounding in their jobs. I recall teaching a course in Scottish *literature* whose students, ardent neo-Celts, persisted in asking me to expound Scottish *history*. Part of the problem is in the teacher: he has not opened the course by explaining and justifying what the course will do, and what it will *not* do. But there is always the student who will not understand or accept this. A middle-aged, amateur theologian—a student whom I like and respect—comes to whatever course I teach because he wants to discuss our theories of Entity. One of my colleagues tells of a student who repeatedly wants to have re-explained a point or problem concluded two weeks ago. Common sense dictates that such dialogues and explanations must be moved to office hours; if the student does not visit (or cannot), that must be his responsibility. But first, I must be sure that the student is an isolated case, or that a discussion of Entity is not what the whole class needs. Most students are obsessed with "relevance" and openly intolerant of any comment or question not immediately "on track." Learning does not happen on a track, and their learning suffers.

But let's return from these nagging common realities to the kinds of questions a teacher of literature might ask, and how to decide whether and when to ask them.

(1) There are, of course, Questions of Fact, and Kasulis recommends them as "warm-up" devices. For the literature teacher, however, it is hard to determine what "fact" about a literary text

is simply factual, and if it is, whether it is important enough to make so prominent. Questions of Fact are better saved and asked as Questions of Evidence, once an issue arises that calls for evidence.

(2) The Summary Question (heresy for old New Critics) serves me better for starters. "Summarize in your own words 'what happens here' however you understand 'happens.' We will test your summary against others' summaries, and try to account for the differences." What I call "summary" is a complex of interpretive acts—call it "translation"—well worth class deliberation. (I do not understand some teachers' denigration of "mere summary" whatever that might be.) It generates lively and productive debate over divergences of order, emphasis, connection, tone.

(3) The Mode of Response Question: "Can you define your reaction to the text, and account for it?" The emphasis here is on *define;* the defining of feelings is difficult at first. The follow-up emphasis is on *account for,* not to be confused with "defend" or "justify." It calls for a description of the process whereby the response grew. For a further follow-up, I collect several different answers from other students, and we then try to explain either a consensus or a division. The discussion easily spills over into a debate of *evaluation,* but I want students to learn that this is a different operation.

(4) The Evaluation Question: "What kind of value does the text have, and how much?" Before answering, we need to choose a scale, a kind of measure, a "criterion" (students may use the word but few understand it).

(5) The Part-Whole Question: "How do parts or elements A and B connect with each other and with the whole work?" This has to be a follow-up question (to summary, response, or evaluation). Otherwise, it invites the student objection (or suspicion) that we are merely "tearing the work apart." The objection is justified; analysis, they must learn, is only a *means* to an end. Likewise . . .

(6) The Exemplification Question: "What is the part or passage an example of? What other examples can you find? [and for

follow-up:] Which is the better example? Are they really examples of the same thing?" Clearly, such a question comes rather late in the process. It calls on the student to identify the general in the particular, to define the general, and to test the definition against other particulars. No mental operation is more fundamental to systematic thinking. It spills over easily into (but should not be confused with) . . .

(7) The Question of Evidence: An example *illustrates;* a piece of evidence *confirms* or supports. Does the student understand the difference?

(8) The Cause-Effect Question: Knowing the notorious difficulty of "causality," I approach this one cautiously. It is significant that most students think of cause as exclusively or chiefly psychological. Their difficulties arise when I ask how psychological causes *differ* from text to text, and when I shift the focus from behavior to event. "Why do Events A and B happen? Is there a causal pattern?" The answering process can be painfully slow, but without it we never come to understand the very nature of "plot." Some students enjoy finessing the question by replying, "Because the writer made it happen!" which then leads into . . .

(9) The Question of Intention: "What did the writer want? Why did she do things this way?" This slippery question is saved for last. It arises inevitably from discussion of cause or motive *in* the text. Even though we can come to no certain answer, the question is extremely useful. Students begin to think of the *writer's* behavior, to think of writing *as* behavior. A few, most notably those who think themselves writers, are ready to think of a text as a series of motivated acts by a person writing. By thinking this way, students can make a quantum jump in how they read.

IV

After all, our question-answer process in class is intended mainly to teach reading. You probably remember Stanley Fish's funny story. A traditionalist colleague met him in the hallway following a first class, and recounted a student's opening question: "Is there a text in this class?" The colleague named a popular anthology. No, replied the student, I mean will we study poems, plays, and novels, or ourselves? The student's question is worth pondering in several of its possible meanings. "Is there a text in this class?" often signifies the most practical curiosities: How expensive is it? How big? How available? How hard or easy, dry or wet? The question also implies more ambiguous queries. Not just "will we use a textbook?" but *how* will we use it? What is its status?

The student is suggesting three underlying questions to the teacher: (1) What is *my* relation to the text supposed to be? (2) What is *your* relation to the text going to be and how will I know it? (3) What is my relation to your relation to the text likely to be and what should I do about it?

In asking such questions, the student is trying initially to "read the teacher," for the teacher is the primary text to be read in any course. What does she *mean?* What does she want? How will I—how am I supposed to—respond to her meanings, aims, wants? How does she operate, why that way, and how must I operate on her operations? Actually, it would be marvelous if students would address the same questions to the texts they are assigned. After all, we learn chiefly from persons. But students often cannot see printed texts as the intended utterances or performances of a real person. Texts seem official, sacrosanct, "completed edifices," reified in prestige. Until they see them as personal acts, their reading will be laborious and ineffectual. Until they do, one of any teacher's primary jobs is to teach them how to read.

To do so, we needn't become experts in the psychodynamics of reading. However, one or two untechnical texts—I think admiringly of Frank Smith's *Reading* (1978), from which some of the points below are derived—would help. Let me remind you of a few relatively uncontroversial points about adult reading.

(1) Reading is an activity that cannot be understood in isola-

tion. To understand reading, Smith writes, you must consider "not just the eyes but also the mechanisms of memory and attention, anxiety, risk-taking, the nature and uses of language, the comprehension of speech, interpersonal relations, sociocultural differences, learning in general" (2). If this inventory seems formidable, it can at least serve to foster tolerance in place of the familiar growl that "students ought to have been taught to read before I got them."

(2) Learning to learn is a lifelong activity. So is learning to read. One is always learning to read better, with a greater variety of responses and comprehension. Whenever one turns to a new kind or level of discourse, one has to adjust one's sense of generic possibilities, become familiar with unfamiliar methods or habits, understand new situations of discourse, revise one's lexicon.

(3) Reading is a transactive process between a text and a reader. In some sense (theorists can argue endlessly about the sense), the meaning in a text can be actualized only in the mind of the reader. The text may be understandable, but only a person can understand it. This does not mean that reading is merely "subjective" or "relative"; rather, it is personal. There will be a range of understandings, emphases, personal priorities, all within the limits of validity (and of course many outside). "The work has structure and meaning because it is read in a particular way. . . . To read a text as literature is not to make one's mind a *tabula rasa* and approach it without preconceptions" (Culler, qtd. in Tompkins 102).

(4) Whatever is understood is understood in a context. Reading to recall cannot be separated from reading to understand, and trying to separate them brings them into conflict. One does not show comprehension by simply repeating what one has read. "We cannot," writes Brownhill, "make a clear distinction between the information we receive and our own judgments about it. Indeed information only becomes information when we assimilate it into our thought patterns, and begin to organize it in a comprehensive way" (37). This is what an author does, and a reader must do it too: to understand is to organize, for organizing is making sense.

(5) Every text is synecdochic and systematic. It includes selective particulars to stand for or illustrate general groups. Its parts represent and belong to a whole. The reader who attends doggedly to particulars without an awareness of what they illustrate or to parts without reference to a whole, cannot understand them. When a student asks us or himself, "What does this mean—this item I am reading?" he may mean one or more of several questions: What is this item here to represent? To what context does it refer? How does it "fit" with other items in the text? What is intended by it—that is, why am I told it? In what way am I supposed to read or understand it? All of these questions call for answers based on something presumably known already.

(6) Every text uses words in its own way. Ambiguity, as Smith says, is "a constant and unavoidable fact of all our language" (72). Key terms, however familiar they may appear, take on new or variant meanings. Learning to read a text is always acquiring a new language. At the same time, reading is always translating a text into one's own words, and translation is always imperfect. We try to understand what we read, as we try to understand anything, by guessing, by predicting. Sometimes we guess wrong; sometimes we remember inaccurately. Students may fail to learn because they are afraid to guess, even though guessing is natural and necessary risk-taking. Mistakes in reading may be extremely meaningful or revealing, and are worth constructive class discussion. Bettelheim and Zolan say, "In responding to the text, the reader digests some of its meaning in an individual and sometimes idiosyncratic manner. . . . A misreading thus represents the person's response to the text and his attempt to communicate this response to himself, to the author, or to anybody listening" (101). Learning a new language requires guessing, risk-taking, learning from mistakes.

(7) Texts for study on assignment are, inevitably, texts to be used. How they are to be used determines how to read them. How to read them determines what questions to ask. The writer writes for a purpose, and the teacher assigns the text for a purpose. Thus "the learner is an archaeologist who is faced with the

problem of finding out the intentions of the people who have produced writing" (Downing 36). If the student is faced with adjusting to the various purposes of the text and of the teacher, and (if he has them) his own, he has a remarkably difficult job to do. He needs help. The help is "teaching him to read."

In assigning a text, we had better begin by recognizing what kinds of difficulties it presents. The familiar phrases students use are elusive but suggestive: "I couldn't get *into* the reading," or "I couldn't get much *out* of it." The two are related: "I couldn't get much out because I couldn't get me in." Students often see a text as an enclosed space with barriers or walls, with doors or windows nonexistent, hidden, or locked. If they do get "inside," they may find a lobby, one room, a closet. They may glimpse other rooms, but can't figure out how to get from one to another, how they're connected. Rather than discovering (that is, understanding) a whole house with a meaningful floor plan, a functional design, they may sense only an arbitrary labyrinth.

If the chief problems are lexical, why not list major terms and phrases? Discuss what meanings we bring to them? Explore how and why they are redefined in the text? If the chief problems are syntactical—problems in making sense of how the text is put together—then begin by identifying parts, and consider how they function relative to each other, why they are positioned as they are. Begin with students' impressions of wholeness and move to parts, or "get in" through parts and move to wholeness. If the chief problems are in understanding the purpose (many texts have complex or shifting purposes) then purpose is the place to begin. But how? Any authorial claim may be unreliable. Claims within the text may be inconstant, partial, or unclear. Two tactics worth trying are: (a) collect guesses of what the purpose might be and test them against the evidence; and (b) present two or three published statements of the text's purpose and debate their relative appropriateness. If the text has notable cruxes, then ask students first to identify passages that give them the most trouble and begin with a diagnosis of why. The diagnosis often leads to a recognition of what is most crucial. It is predictable that many students will identify the same passages.

The second question to ask when assigning a text is how will it affect the course as a whole. Will prior texts and discussions prepare the way? Will succeeding texts clarify or reinforce? Avoid placing especially difficult texts too early or too late. Put the most difficult texts in the middle (the precision stage). An especially difficult text at the start of a course is likely to be lost forever; placed at the end, it is sure to get perfunctory, weary attention.

Third, what should you do to prepare for, without overdetermining, the reading? There are many priming possibilities, all of them intended to offer a "way in." One is to dramatize the text: construct a lively image of the author's situation in writing. Another is to frame the reading in issues or divergent viewpoints. Some texts do not lend themselves to such argumentative treatment, and other kinds of priming are better. If there is a difficult central concept, explore it with the class ahead of time. Extract a few key terms and have students share their own definitions, so that when they encounter the text's definitions, they will be alerted to the need for redefinition. If the text's difficulties are structural, structural priming is called for. Identify in advance one passage midway through the text, and ask students to figure out its importance and its location, to explain how the author "got there" from the beginning. Or, pick in advance one early page and have students explain what would have been missing from their reading had that page been left out or lost.

All of these tactical possibilities share one aim: to help get the class into the text and the text into the class. In this, they differ in emphasis from Robert Scholes's recent thoughts on the teaching of reading, as we see in "The Text in the Class," from his book *Textual Power*.

Our obligation, Scholes argues (and I agree), is to help students learn to make their own texts, constructs of what they read. Reading and making cannot be independent of each other. Scholes would teach reading in three stages. The first he calls "reading proper," the second "interpretation," and the third "criticism." In reading proper, we make sense of the particular structures in the text, and make the text "within" the text. To do this we must recognize what kind of text it is, its generic "code." In the second stage, interpretation, we move to "generalized themes and values" and try to understand the text's value code. Third, we move to criticism of that code and make our text "against" the text. Scholes's book places strong emphasis on this final stage.

I like the inductive direction of the scheme. I like his insistence that interpretation is not *all* readers do and not all *we* as teachers should offer. I admire his insistence that "reading proper" (analytic summary, for example) matters, and that critical powers must be cultivated. But I am bothered by three things. First, his distinctions overlap. Second, reading cannot move in such an orderly linear process, and third, we should not teach as if it could. Teaching reading has to begin in a different place: not "in" the text, but in the process, the response to it. The response is partly interpretive, partly critical. We begin with the text as an act of reading and an act of writing.

Two points in opposition are worth emphasizing. First, Scholes's distinction between reading and interpretation is elusive. We cannot make sense of mere reading without some generalizing, some "thematizing." When I ask students to summarize, I am asking them to perform interpretive acts. Second, criticism does not wait upon the completion of reading-interpreting. One does not submit and then resist. Without some opposition, some active questioning, reading and interpretation cannot happen. The activity of critical engagement is needed to realize what we read, to "get into it." The process has to work in and out and in again. Critical dialogue with what we read is as much a way in as a way out. Our first pedagogical aim is to "get readers in."

V

How will we know and judge how far in our students got, and how much they got out of the reading? Part of every class event, whether we like it or not, is evaluation. Evaluating student learning is separate from—in some respect inimical to—teaching. But unless I evaluate learning, I cannot teach effectively. Evaluation is measurement according to some norm or scale. When I evaluate a student (the student's work? can I really separate them?), how do I measure? One must answer for oneself, and then somehow adjust the personal answer to the collective answers of discipline and institution.

The problem is illuminated by the modern distinction between competence and performance, *langue* and *parole*. Competence is the whole system of the student's knowledge of a subject matter. Performance is what, on some occasion, the student is able to perform of that knowledge-understanding.

Some would argue that a student's competence is defined as what the student can perform, but this is doubtful. We all understand some ideas, structures, acts without being able to perform them. In some courses, performance is what must be measured, for performance—writing, language use, method—is what is taught. In others, what counts is the student's acquisition of organized knowledge. In literature, the performance we are inclined (rightly or wrongly) to be most interested in is what we call Good Reading, but Good Reading is not a performance we can observe. We can only infer it from other kinds of performance.

Whatever we may believe about the connections between knowing and communicating, we have had students about whom we had to say, "He understood the material well, I think, but he could not express it well." We have said of others, "She wrote well or made interesting, clear statements, but I think she did not understand the material as well as some who wrote or spoke less effectively." And then we had to struggle, often irrationally, with the problem of how to evaluate. We need a more rational, principled way to decide.

In the teaching of literature, the decision made long ago was this: the student is to become a Good Critic and must perform well in the kind of discourse called the critical paper. Many of us, unsettled about the nature of criticism, still use the critical paper, and still teach required courses whose end is "writing about literature," with textbooks to match. Some have escaped from this narrow model, only to cling to a broader version. The student of literature must perform well in expository writing. In a culture obsessed with "writing," it is sometimes easy to forget

that the end of literary study is competence in reading, understanding, thinking about literature, and that writing, while essential, must remain a means to that end.

What kinds of written performance are most likely to further
that competence, and to reveal it best for evaluation? The answer
has to be: kinds of performance that come closest to the actual processes of reading and thinking. Some teachers assign what they
call "informal response papers"; the student sets down in no particular shape a description of personal responses. How much can
be learned from this? Mere response generates no further, more
precise learning. Others assign a course journal, and ideally such
a performance should teach and reveal much. But the course
journal is an artifice difficult for many to handle. Once I observed
a teacher trying to explain the "journal assignment." To whom,
asked a student, should the journal be written? To yourself, answered the teacher, but I will read it! Moreover, the journal belongs to a sophisticated stage of development; it is what Vygotsky
calls "inner speech," talking reflectively to oneself, translated
into writing. We need forms of writing that are more occasional,
more closely integrated with the collective learning of a class.

Two such forms of performance have worked well for me: the
short, in-class process writing and the class letter. In the first,
spontaneity and immediacy are what make for revelation. We
"catch" the student in the process of shared deliberation. Perhaps we open class with this for five or ten minutes: "Summarize
the main conclusion we reached last time." (Some summaries are
compared and the differences accounted for.) Or we interrupt
midway with: "The issue at this point seems to be . . . Write
down where you stand on it now, and why." (The discussion then
reopens upon this polarization.) Or we close class with: "In the
final five or six minutes, describe the main problem of reading for
you that was *not* solved today." These writings belong to the process of deliberation and advance it, while clarifying the student's
mind and enlightening the teacher's.

The class letter is a performance of a different kind. It comes
close to conversation; it is addressed to the group as an act of
communication; problems of audience are reduced and dialogue

develops. The task is to explain to the group one significant problem the student has had in reading the text, to describe how that problem developed, how it felt, and to make a focused request for assistance. Samples are read and discussed. Repeated practice in the letter form should develop into journalizing as the student grows more accustomed to the roles of speaker-writer and listener-reader simultaneously. I require the student to keep all letters with my brief letters of response, to review them, to revise if she wishes, and to resubmit the portfolio at the end as a tracing of the development of reading and thinking throughout the course. This permits me a continuous process of biweekly revelations, and at the end, I can review my own past assessments against a final rereading. How much time does this take the teacher? Four hours to "answer" each set of letters, and my answers provide excellent material for class preparation.

I have no illusions about the relations between a good letter and the performance of a formal paper. Am I shirking my responsibility in not "teaching the paper"? I think not. The paper is not the course's objective. The paper as performance is not a reliable and continuing index of learning, and so I use it sparingly.

My final exam is different in what it requires and reveals. I choose short passages from the course texts and distribute them in advance. We discuss a few briefly. In Part I, the student is asked to identify and define what he considers important exemplary characteristics of any kind in each *passage*. In Part II, he is asked to construct his own essay question, based on similarities he has observed in three or four of the passages, and then to write the essay. The results give an unusually full revelation not only of what the student knows, but also of how she can think with that knowledge, perceive and describe patterns, exemplify and generalize.

Some students perform well on the exam and others on the letters. The best letter writers are able to focus and explain their own processes as readers; their strengths are deductive, inferential. The best exam writers are more inductive, experimental. They begin with a more attentive openness to the implications of various materials and proceed more cautiously to generalization.

The first are stronger thinkers; the second are more attentive readers. The student coming closest to the combined ideal receives the best grade.

The general problem is that our testing instruments must serve too many functions. We want students to learn from doing them. We want the instruments to show us what learning is going on and where the difficulties are. We need them to certify the level of competence the student has reached. No instrument can be designed well to fulfill all three functions at once. How can a student learn, reveal, and perform at the same time? We must decide on each occasion what matters most and design accordingly. And the same choosing of priorities, the same careful design, applies to all elements that make up the text and performance of a class session.

THREE

The Strangeness of Learning to Learn

I

Naturally, while we are evaluating our students' learning, they are evaluating our teaching. An anxious fellow, I often ask for their evaluations round about midterm. Here is one of the most staggering and intriguing midway reviews I ever received (emphasis added):

Question: What is the most valuable aspect of this course as a learning experience so far?

Answer: *Exploration* of different views and ideas. This *expands* my ways of thinking and helps me look at *others'* views instead of *relying* on my own which can be *dangerous*.

Question: What is your chief problem or difficulty with the course so far?

Answer: Lack of *cohesiveness*. The course does not seem to *follow a direction*. The classes are well prepared, but I'm not sure *what the goal is* or should be. I don't feel I have a grasp on what *the teacher wants* or what *I'm learning*.

Question: What kinds of things are you learning most? Information? Ideas? Ways of thinking? Methods of learning? Other?

Answer: I'm afraid I don't feel I am learning very much. I like how the class *explores ideas* (except when I disagree with somebody) but the class *reminds me of a philosophy class.* I find it *frustrating.*

Question: What features of the way the course is taught are most helpful to you? What change in teaching would you most want the teacher to make?

Answer: I'd like more *specifics* on what *makes* an adventure. I'd like to know what *themes* relate the books, what *common ideas* make them adventures. I find the class well prepared and well thought out.

To understand the student's problem, we must recall what was going on in class. The course might once have been labeled a beginning humanities course. It provided one method for beginning the study of literature. In texts of various kinds from many cultures and periods, we studied a basic kind of experience, perhaps the most archaic and universal of all: adventure. The stage of learning was the one Whitehead calls "romance" (but "adventure" suits just as well). The aim was helping students learn to learn. The subject was literature in its strangeness, its definitive value.

Let me briefly summarize our questioning of three episodes from three texts: first, the raft Kon-Tiki crossing the dangerous reef to the south sea island beach; second, Odysseus's climactic struggle to survive cliff and whirlpool, Scylla and Charybdis; third, Robinson Crusoe's triumphant discovery that he could make an earthenware pot. I need not transcribe the actual dialogue to make my point.

Part I: Let's begin with the most obvious feeling that the episodes share: excitement. The people having these experiences are unusually excited, and perhaps the reader is, too. What is it that makes each experience so exciting? Something in the people? In us? In the situations? All three? Let's look at the experiences and see what they are made of, how they are shaped. [The aim is to discover that an experience has a shape and that its shape generates its meaning.]

Part II: Each is a time set apart. What makes its begin-
                ning? What makes its ending? How long does it
                last? What does time feel like here, and how is
                time measured? Do we normally measure time
                differently? Why is timing so important for the
                Kon-Tiki crew as they ride the wave, or for Odys-
                seus as he leaps, grabs, and jumps again? or for
                Crusoe as he fires his pot? Think of situations in
                your own experience when timing was crucial.

Part III: Timing depends on knowing where you are.
                What is strange about these places? What makes
                each of the adventurers so much at home in these
                places? Notice how each of them reads the signs
                around him and uses what he learns to handle his
                environment.

Part IV: We move from the *when* and the *where* to the
                why. Why do these episodes happen? Why do
                they end in success? Is it all chance? Are laws
                operating too? [What's the difference?] How could
                Odysseus possibly survive such dangers? How
                could the Kon-Tiki crew? How could one naive
                man alone on an island do what Crusoe does?
                When you say that there is something you cannot
                possibly do, how are you measuring possibility?

Part V: Succeeding against impossible odds in strange
                places demands certain kinds of behavior. There
                is a right way to act, a code. What codes of be-
                havior are being acted out, and what makes them
                the right ones? Do the codes have anything in
                common? Each of our adventurers is being
                tested, and each passes his test. What is being
                tested here?

Part VI: The three experiences have extraordinary value
                for the adventurers. A value is an idea of what
                matters, what is desirable—wealth, security,
                fame, pleasure, whatever. What makes each of
                these experiences valuable? Does Odysseus care

most about physical survival? Does Heyerdahl simply want to get ashore? Does Crusoe rejoice because now he can cook a meal? Do their values have anything in common?

Part VII: Whatever other value one gets from an adventure—as a doer, or as a reader—one of its values is in what one learns. What is learned from each of these episodes? How is it learned? Do *you* learn anything valuable?

The student who filled out the above evaluation was not ready to discover such patterns. He lacked the confidence of the adventurer in confronting strangeness and employing ideas to make meaningful shapes; he wanted me to provide the conceptual patterns ready-framed and defined. He had not yet learned how to learn. What is needed? How can it be gained?

Probably the best account I have read of the process of learning to learn occurs in a true adventure story of the Australian desert, *Tracks* (1980). Alone on camel-back, a young ex-secretary named Robyn Davidson is learning from the desert:

And as I walked through that country, I was becoming involved with it in a most intense and yet not fully conscious way. The motions and patterns and connections of things became apparent on a gut level. I didn't just *see* the animal tracks, I *knew* them. I didn't just *see* the bird, I knew it in relationship to its actions and effects. My environment began to teach me about itself without my full awareness of the process. It became an animate being of which I was a part. The only way I can describe how the process occurred is to give an example: I would see a beetle's tracks in the sand. What once would have been merely a pretty visual design with a few associations attached, now became a sign which produced in me instantaneous associations—the type of beetle, which direction it was going in and why, when it made the tracks, who its predators were. *Having been taught some rudimentary knowledge of the pattern of things at the beginning of the trip, I now had enough to provide a structure in*

which I could learn to learn. . . . . What was once a thing that
merely existed became something that everything else acted
upon and had a relationship with and vice versa. . . . When
this way of thinking became ordinary for me, I too became
lost in the net and the boundaries of myself stretched out for
ever. (emphasis added, 195)

What does it mean to become intensely involved with a
strange place? If it is a country of the mind, how can we teachers
generate such involvement? To notice on the level of physical
awareness, to notice motion and pattern, is where learning begins. How can we teach an awareness of pattern? We keep asking, "Do you sense any connections?" Knowing, as Davidson
says, is more than seeing; it is seeing relationships. What does
any teacher mean when she asks the student, "Do you see what I
mean?" if not, "Do you see the connections in what I said?" How
can we teach seeing connections? We encourage the notion of
wholeness; we discourage seeing anything in isolation. We keep
asking, "What is the context?"

Davidson is being taught by a new environment. How can
we make a new subject into an environment (as novelists do)?
What tactics best immerse, best draw the student in? We must
find the liveliest point of contact and use it as a doorway. For
Davidson, it is a process. How do we teach a process? It comes by
example. What is an example? No process is more important for
students to learn than exemplification. Again and again we ask
the student to perform an act: "Give me an example." And then,
always, we follow up: "What is that an example of? What makes it
a good example?"

Davidson is learning because she is asking different kinds of
questions—not just what, but what type, which direction, why,
when, who. How do we teach students to ask many kinds of questions? By doing so ourselves and asking them to do likewise. She
learns through signs. Do our students know what a sign is? They
live surrounded by signs. They must learn to see every new phenomenon as a sign. Even a desert is filled with signs. We need
tracking devices. Would we turn a student loose in the desert

with no tracking devices? Davidson has been provided with a rough map. What kind of a map shall we give? At the start of our "trip," students ask, "What shall I look for, and where?" If I reply, "Find out for yourself," I am not doing enough. But if I give a finished map, they never learn to map for themselves. Teaching any subject is teaching map-making. "Draw me a map of what you learned last week" is a good assignment.

Knowing is recognizing. To know a thing is to recognize it in its context. How shall we teach so that learning becomes a process of building contexts? "Let me give you the context" is going too far; "find your own context" gives nothing to build with. We say, "Here are a few pieces. See if you can tell me how they are a context for what we are looking at—this bird, this word, this idea." Then the building starts. A new way of thinking—call it contextualism—becomes a habit. A new habit expands the self, makes knowing personal. Davidson's is a habit of attention. Because Davidson in the desert is interacting with her environment, she is attentive. Attention is both active and passive.

Where do we find the kind of attentiveness we want to cultivate? Models are everywhere, and we blunder if we ignore them. We find our students passionately attentive when they are involved in games, in gambling, in lovemaking, in playacting, in mapping and making by rule and recipe, in adventure. What have all these in common? Risk, suspense, uncertainty. Practical engineering, detecting signs, reading codes. Self-surrender, imagination, speculation. These are powers to be cultivated, and cultivation is a process both active and passive. It does things, gives things, but it watches and listens, too, attends on things. In chapter 7 of *Biographia Literaria*, Coleridge says,

> Most of my readers will have observed a small water-insect on the surface of rivulets . . . and will have noticed how the little animal wins its way up against the stream, by alternate pulses of active and passive motion, now resisting the current, and now yielding to it in order to gather strength and a momentary fulcrum for a further propulsion. This is no unapt emblem of the mind's self-experience in the act of thinking.

There are evidently two powers at work, which, relatively to each other, are active and passive; and this is not possible without an intermediate faculty, which is at once both active and passive . . . the IMAGINATION. (174–5)

This is no inapt emblem of learning. Those small water-insects, our students, are on the stream, now resisting, now yielding. And who are we? Not, certainly, benevolent hands to carry them along. But not mere spectators, either, watching from the banks. We are the keepers of the sluice gates. We try to guide the stream. This is the active and the passive of our calling.

II

Here, in this predisciplinary core or General Education course, we must begin. It is terribly difficult to decide how much, and how best, to guide the stream at this stage. It is easy to go to one extreme or another in our pedagogies, our styles. At one extreme is the pedagogical persona I call the Torpedo Fish; at the other, the Person from Porlock. In moderated forms, both are needed. The Torpedo Fish may serve well at the predisciplinary or romance stage (as we see it in this chapter). In Chapter Four, a modified Person from Porlock takes over as we move into the second or precision stage. In Chapter Five, we will need yet another persona for a third or "contextual" stage. But please recognize that this dramatis personae sounds too simple. The stages are neither separate nor mutually exclusive, and the three personae enter and exit and interact throughout the process.

My poor student of the midcourse review was feeling torpedoed. The teacher as Torpedo Fish, you may recall, was Socrates querying poor Meno about what could be taught until Meno felt bewildered, torpified. The teacher as Person from Porlock is drawn from that legendary anonymity who interrupted Coleridge in the creation of "Kubla Khan." Both are wakeners, as teachers ought to be; both are intruders, as teachers must be. The Torpedo Fish wakens from unexamined certitudes and often generates desperate confusion. The Person from Porlock wakens from enchanted absorption and reasserts the familiar world. Both are dangerous, and both may be indispensable, carefully managed in their exits and entrances.

The Torpedo Fish is easily defended in the abstract. Stephen David Ross offers a defense most of us could subscribe to:

> learning and inquiry are frequently confusing and paralyzing in certain phases. . . . A change in paradigm, logical system, or general viewpoint is required, and this will frequently produce confusion where the transition from one organizing perspective to another is involved. . . . (10)

A fundamental challenge to one's vision of the world is paralyzing; yet one will learn from it only by pushing on. Schooling for most people is either the routine acquisition of facts, without the paralysis of a challenged vision, or the easy acquisition of untrammeled insights. Such students are ill-equipped to confront the possibility of a transcendence in vision which all significant learning requires. (37)

If significant learning demands the confronting of new and strange points of view, however bewildering the process, then we must sometimes be Torpedo Fish. Especially so, if we believe that literature ought to challenge one's vision of the world, that literature works by defamiliarization, revealing the strangeness of the familiar. But some literary texts do so more radically. The possibilities of transcendence or transformation in vision, in viewpoint, are what they are all about. Let's consider the teaching of three such texts, "Rime of the Ancient Mariner," *Gulliver's Travels*, and *The Tempest*, in a first core course in literature.

Teaching such texts involves teaching some fundamentals of point of view—not, mind you, in the narrow "literary" sense of fictional rhetoric. A point of view is a way of organizing experience, a form of thought, a mode or system of belief (see Brownhill 26). How will our students discover and adopt the modes of belief that give meaning to such texts as these? Are they willing to suppose that one could see the world filled with tutelary spirits, governed by supernatural mystery? Or that the world could be seen as inhabited by petty marionettes, gross giants, wise horses, and depraved humanoid Yahoos? Or seen as governed by magic, witchcraft, and a power that can effect redemption by mysterious "natural" agencies? The teacher as Person from Porlock can help them to familiar interpretive categories.

The Person from Porlock is often defended as the teacher who imparts critical processes and methods, intercedes in imaginative response with the categories and instruments of analysis and evaluation. Edward Partridge offers a balanced defense:

> Everyone has to read a poem as though it were a love letter to him: slowly, alone, in full surrender to it. Yet even as one surrenders to a work or enters fully into it (either metaphor will do), some critical process, however unsystematic and even unconscious it may be, has already begun. . . . So far as teaching is concerned, it is impossible to separate the experience of literature from the criticism of it. (51)

Our willingness to agree depends, of course, on what is meant by criticism. In fact, Partridge seems inconsistent. At first, "As a critic—and any reader is a critic—one tries to discover the unique experience of a work and to judge the value of that experience" (52). Fine. Criticism is simply study that seeks to identify a literary experience and then to evaluate it by some standard. But must the standard for judging the experience come from "literary theory," theory that "concerns itself both with the kind of literature a work is and with the standards by which one ought properly to judge it" (52)? This is a rather narrow idea of literary theory; moreover, it shifts attention from discovering and evaluating the experience to classifying and judging the work.

Partridge cites Northrop Frye as authority: "To him experience and study must reciprocally affect each other, the direct experience purifying literary study of pedantry, the judicious study purifying experience of stock responses" (51). Fine. But Frye describes the timing differently. There is the "direct experience" which is "pre-critical" or "uncritical." Then there is "the conscious, critical response we make *after we've finished* reading or left the theatre, where we compare what we've experienced with other things of the same kind, and form a judgment of value and proportion on it," relating it ultimately to "our literary experience as a whole, as a total possession" (*Educated Imagination* 104, emphasis added). The issue, then, is not whether criticism plays a role, but when and what kind. Partridge quotes Barbara Hardy (NB a midsixties statement):

> the experience of art is a thing of our making, an activity in which we are our own interpretative artist. The dryness of schematic analysis of imagery, symbols, myth, structural relations, *et al.* should be avoided passionately at school and often at college. *It is literature, not literary criticism which is the subject.* (51)

The confusion is not limited to literature. R. J. Brownhill recalls a first-year philosophy course (my own was identical) in which the teacher introduced Descartes critically, with the result that students asked why such a trivial and mistaken philosopher was deemed worthy of study. "A pupil has to be shown round a subject, and begin to understand it before he ever criticizes it. Early criticism can, for a pupil, destroy a subject before it has got off the ground" (49–50). The problem is what sort of showing round can clarify and strengthen. The tension we must cope with is between two worthy goals in the study of literature: the enlargement of self-surrender, self-transcendence; the strengthening of discipline. Can we enlarge and discipline the imagination at more or less the same time? The answer depends on what we mean by discipline. Ursula K. LeGuin has an eloquent answer:

> To be free, after all, is not to be undisciplined. I should say that the discipline of the imagination may in fact be the essential method or technique of both art and science. It is our Puritanism, insisting that discipline means repression or punishment, which confuses the subject. To discipline something, in the proper sense of the word, does not mean to repress it, but to train it—to encourage it to grow, and act, and be fruitful, whether it is a peach tree or a human mind. (*The Language of the Night* 41)

We will attempt to discover what she means and whether her ideal is feasible.

But first, recall one more attack, a classic by now, on "criticism" in teaching. The attack pervades C. S. Lewis's provocative 1961 tract *An Experiment in Criticism.* It is grounded in his distinctions between Good Reading and Bad Reading. The Bad Reader is one who merely "uses" all he reads for his own prior interests, one who is always busy "doing things with the work." The Good Reader is one who "receives" the work and has something "done to him." To receive, we must surrender ourselves first, without asking whether the work justifies such surrender, for if we do not surrender first, we cannot find out. We need to see with other eyes, imagine with other imaginations, feel with other hearts. The greatest value in Good Reading is the experience of self-enlargement, and this must begin with self-surrender.

Some teachers will applaud such a position as self-evidently admirable. Others will reject it as a frontal attack on the most current of pedagogies: active reading, critical thinking, a constant "doing things" to what we read, imposing our questions and categories upon it. Both groups might well find Lewis's position "romantic," as indeed it is, for it belongs to a tradition that stretches from the German Romantics through Coleridge and Newman, through Dilthey and George Herbert Mead, to the modern philosopher of science Michael Polanyi. It holds that knowing is personal, that to know something we must be "in" it, that understanding the clues of perception, as Polanyi says, requires that we immerse ourselves in them, "dwell in" them, become committed, even obsessed, in our "indwelling."

The self-surrender, self-transcendence, which Lewis hopes for sounds remarkably close to Keats's ideal of the Poetical Character. Its critical faculties are suspended in Negative Capability— the capacity of "being in uncertainties, Mysteries, doubts, without any irritable reaching after fact and reason." The Keatsian version will prove germane to our teaching, especially when seen beside what Coleridge wrote about the conception of "The Ancient Mariner":

> the incidents and agents were to be, in part at least, supernatural; and the excellence aimed at was to consist in the interesting of the affections by the dramatic truth of such emotions, as would naturally accompany such situations,

supposing them real. . . . my endeavors should be directed to persons and characters supernatural, or at least romantic; yet so as to transfer from our inward nature a human interest and a semblance of truth sufficient to procure for these shadows of imagination that willing suspension of disbelief for the moment, which constitutes poetic faith. (264)

The key terms for our concerns are "supposing" and "belief." Our first job is to explore questions of belief with our students. Do we *suppose* the Mariner's situation to be real, and what is meant by "suppose"? Can we share the Mariner's belief in being under supernatural agency? Can we share the wonder of a Ferdinand, a Miranda, or a Gulliver? Can we follow through their experiences of strangeness or mystery without "an irritable reaching after fact and reason"? If we do not believe as we read, if we read without surrender, how can we understand, how can we learn? Must not the teacher himself suspend disbelief? If not, how can students find a genuine access? Can wonder be learned?

The dilemma for the teacher is real. It is posed well by Partridge's gloss on Bradley's "Poetry for Poetry's Sake." Bradley argues that the nature of any literary work is to be "a world by itself, independent, complete, autonomous; and to possess it fully you must enter that world, conform to its law, and ignore for the time the beliefs, aims, and particular conditions which belong to you in the other world of reality." Partridge wants to have it both ways. "Though," he says, "we must ignore the other world of reality in some radical aesthetic sense, we must draw on it continuously" (50). What can this mean? All three of our texts radically challenge familiar beliefs, familiar ways of looking at things. The kind of learning that takes place *in* the works is learning that arouses wonder and amazement, demands self-enlargement through self-surrender. Can the reader experience this defamiliarizing, this shock of wonder without which discovery is impossible, and at the same time draw continuously on the familiar as the means of understanding?

Here is a basic paradox in learning and teaching. True knowledge of the works requires a surrender to their strangeness. Otherwise, we will simply impose our own points of view, familiar structures and categories. But how do we get "in"? We need a way of access, starting from the familiar outside—risking what Lewis dislikes. Every imaginative text is a relearning of the world. If students are to learn, I must help them assimilate unfamiliar worlds to their own patterns of thought and belief. But if the works do not powerfully challenge and even modify those patterns, convey strange, new ways of organizing experience, then I haven't *taught* them at all, and new patterns cannot have been learned, at least not in Polanyi's sense of "personal knowledge."

So in the teaching of such texts, the aspect of literary value or response called "believability" demands study and discussion. We must ask how the unbelievable becomes believable, the impossible possible. It is risky to raise such questions, for we cannot do so without compelling students to examine and speak about their own beliefs. In doing so, we cannot remain neutral or reticent about our own beliefs, for that would be unethical, or worse, bad pedagogy. If we follow through on such a radical plan, we are sure to be Torpedo Fish. If not, we are mere Persons from Porlock.

The most offensively Porlockian beginning would be to find such fables odd, peopled by quaint beliefs, but "interesting" as allegory or myth to be interpreted into testable propositions about psychic states or archetypes. (Coleridge's talk about "delusion" and "transfer" from "our inward nature" brings him perilously close to such a position.) This is to transfer the whole question of belief from reading to interpretation: the issue becomes not the experience of the text, but the believability of the interpretation.

A slightly less Porlockian beginning would be to approach these "fables" by way of intellectual history: the Elizabethan World Picture of *The Tempest*, the Augustan of *Gulliver's Travels*, the Romantic of the "Mariner." It wouldn't be a bad idea to end up with such historical perspective on different ways of viewing the world. But to do this first is to impose a screen of conceptual systems between the reader's primary experience and the experience in the texts. And if we do not begin with the experience of strangeness and wonder, we go nowhere.

Or we could begin with a generic context. Suppose we accept W. R. Irwin's definition of fantasy and ask whether any of the texts is "true fantasy"? Or Tolkien's view that the reader of fantasy retains a firm sense of the difference between possibility and impossibility, and gives a credence that is purely playful, speculative? Or Todorov's positioning of fantasy on a continuum of genres—the uncanny, the fantastic, the marvelous—and ask how to position our texts accordingly? If we do, we discover that our students have no notion of what makes a genre or mode, where such definitions come from, or what uses they have for a reader. The objections are thoroughly explained by Brownhill:

> We could be taught a comprehensive pattern, although it could be argued that a pattern perceived in this way may not be perceived in exactly the way the teacher expects. In order to teach a pattern a teacher would have to specify certain concepts about primary facts so that the pupil could understand how the pattern could be made to emerge, and then gradually indicate the connecting links between different facts in order to create the comprehensive picture. . . . The teaching method . . . which Polanyi in fact advocates [NB in the teaching of science], is that the pupil or rather apprentice should, as far as possible, be led to find his own patterns. That is the teacher should try and give the apprentice the skill to make his own discoveries within the existing traditions of the enterprise. (41–42)

This is the disciplining of the imagination. This is learning to learn.

Much more fundamental and generative than learning *about* a certain genre or mode is the discovery that there *are* such concepts, that they matter, that they play an active role in learning. The best way to discover this is *to guide students through the process of inventing such a concept*. We begin with three texts in which experiences of strangeness and wonder occur, and ask what seems most strange or wonderful in each, with the aim of discovering what wonder and strangeness may be. We ask for important resemblances and differences, move from specific comparisons to more general ones, and finally to the notion of literary kinds. And last we *name* what we have invented. Whenever I have followed this process, the class has finally invented a definition of a genre or a mode at least as good as any in the glossaries.

III

Begin then with the obvious. All three works take people from familiar realities to strange worlds, confront them with strangeness, with worlds that operate by different laws, and in so doing challenge and perhaps transform their beliefs. All three send their amazed travelers home again. In what state do they return? In what state do we? When Shakespeare closes his illusion with assurances that we are all illusory and life a play, is this our homecoming vision or belief? When Gulliver returns with a distorted vision that divides him from his own humanity, is this our homecoming vision? When the Mariner returns cleansed but tied forever to his penance, what of us? Are we the wedding guest, forced for a time to listen and believe, but never to voyage on such fantastic journeys?

We begin with the Mariner and ask for a consensual summary of his experience—its stages, climaxes, and connections. We turn to his compulsive tale-telling and ask for possible causes: Why would a person who has had an extraordinary or unbelievable experience feel compelled to tell you his story? If you are the wedding guest, how do you feel? What kinds of happenings do you anticipate? We focus on three qualities that make the Mariner's story strange: (1) how things happen to him; (2) how he sees them; and (3) how others see him. What kinds of happenings, and why do they happen? Why do situations change so suddenly? Why is the albatross welcomed? Why does the Mariner shoot him? Why is he punished? The Person from Porlock would await rational answers; the Torpedo Fish would persist in showing that there are none. If, says Polanyi, we insist on imposing on strange phenomena our own "artificial pattern of cause and effect," we miss the patterns we seek. We need to discover that there are different ways of explaining things. The mystery of the way things happen here—suddenly, inexplicably, disjointedly—has to be confronted.

The first thing that fixes us to the Mariner is his eye. He is an eye-witness; we believe him because he has seen what he tells; we should explore what eye-witness means. Seeing is most of what he does; he sees in different ways; his seeing changes. Where do we see the change and its effects most dramatically? Our discussion will focus on the climax of part 4, where slimy things are suddenly seen as "happy living things" and "blessed unaware." He *awakens to a new way of seeing*, and this awakening is what our students must come to experience. We are asked to discover a sacramental vision of the world through the awakening of the Mariner's vision and to realize its redemptive power.

But why the Mariner? This too is a mystery. Others do not see this way. How does the crew differ in their ways of seeing and explaining things? Back, finally, to the wedding guest. Do his reactions change or grow, and what is the final effect as he too awakens? What is the nature of his sadness, of the wisdom he has gained? Are our reactions guided by his? "The poet," one reader has argued, "wants us to play the part of the wedding guest, to be drawn into the poem unwillingly, to resist with the understanding, and finally to share his epistemological and perhaps also, for the readers who can still do so, his religious anxieties" (Boulger 446). If, as I believe, this is so, then the tale tries our beliefs and our capacities for vision, and its teaching must explore these trials if students are to learn to learn.

IV

Following "The Ancient Mariner," *Gulliver's Travels* must seem strange, and part of our aim is to discover how such a context of readings shapes our expectations. This, too, is learning to learn. Here, too, we are in the hands of a strange teller. Yet, at the start no one could seem more matter-of-fact than Gulliver. Then comes the first storm at sea, and he sleeps, and awakens to wonder. Wonder is the reiterated key word.

Porlockian introducers seldom fail to remind us that we are supposed to have enjoyed and wondered at *Gulliver's Travels* as naive children, but that we are children no longer. What was a charming fantasy of "circumstantial magic" (Cunliffe xvi) now has terrible intimations and has become a book of satiric horror. Invalidating the "childlike" response, will they lose something essential and short-circuit the primary experience of surrender to the book? I think so. Without the wonder, the ridiculous cannot properly emerge. Students can learn much about themselves as readers if they recognize the thin line between the wonderful and the ridiculous.

The book displays a series of episodes of discovery, of awakening to wonder, of forced shifts in ways of seeing. Our teaching might begin with such episodes, moments when strangers from strange worlds confront each other in wonder, feel amazement, and attempt to make sense in ways familiar to them. But what happens is defamiliarizing: the familiar is seen in a strange, new way. For some, this is the nature of all discovery and learning. For others, it is the fundamental strategy of art. That the defamiliarizing reveals reality in a way that is satiric, or fantastic, is a matter of specific application. But first, students need to realize the fundamental process.

Ask, then, what kinds of strangeness are experienced and what kinds of wondering go on. A few examples of many: Gulliver eats in front of the Lilliputians, who show a "thousand marks of wonder and astonishment," and when he has "performed these wonders" they dance on his chest, causing him to "wonder at the intrepidity of these diminutive mortals." Brobdingnagian scholars seek in vain to explain tiny Gulliver, can find no "causes" for him, and invent the "wonderful solution" of calling him a *lusus naturae*, a sport of nature. (What explanation might *we* invent? Have a comparative look back at the ways the crew views the Mariner.) Sailing home from Brobdingnag, Gulliver is observed by the captain "to look at everything with a sort of wonder, and that I often seem hardly able to contain my laughter, which he knew not well how to take, but imputed it to some disorder in my brain. I answered, it was very true; and I wondered how I could forbear. . . ." Gulliver is inspected by the Houyhnhnms "with manifest tokens of wonder," "new signs of wonder," while he is "amazed" to see animals behaving in ways "so orderly and rational, so acute and judicious."

The idea of the strange differs from that in the "Mariner." We are jolted or disoriented in different ways. Our beliefs are challenged differently. Which do our students find more challenging or unbelievable: a world inhabited by tutelary spirits or a world inhabited by giants, Lilliputians, and wise, talking horses? Why? That question from the Torpedo Fish should get us to the heart of the matter of belief.

Strangeness in *Gulliver* depends initially on scale and proportion. What is not in proportion with the "familiar" seems a wonder, a marvel. The further we read, the more familiar it becomes. The more familiar it seems, the more we as readers make references back to familiar reality and become aware that this process creates amusement. It is funny to have "one of us" behaving like a Lilliputian, and funny to have Lilliputians behaving like "us." We say it is "ridiculous." We are discovering satire, as already we have discovered fantasy.

But as with fantasy, so now with satire; rather than impose definitive concepts, we will do better to explore the fundamental responses of which they are made. What do we mean by "incongruous" and by "ridiculous"? Can things seem either wonderful or ridiculous according to our way of looking at them? In Book Three, what general strangeness do these creatures share, and what general expectations make them ridiculous? From these we can infer the standards by which they are being measured. And when we have collected such patterns, we have invented a genre or mode and can name it. This is learning to learn.

In Book Four, the word "wonderful" has given way to "monstrous" and "unnatural." (We may want to explore such terms, in anticipation of their importance for Shakespeare.) When we reach the final book our problems of *belief* have altered drastically. Is Swift suggesting that horses are wiser than men? That would seem unbelievable. Is he declaring that men ought to be like these animals? Some might refuse to believe such a declaration, but "belief" means something different here. Is he asserting that humans are Yahoos, or are *like* Yahoos, or *can be seen as* Yahoos? Actually, the alteration in Gulliver's way of seeing has brought him to this, and the final chapters focus on his altered vision. What shall we make of it? This is, of course, the ultimate crux in Gulliver criticism, but our introductory teaching need not resolve it to a scholarly degree.

We agree that Gulliver seems strange and ridiculous to most readers. And if my students and I have managed to invent an idea of the ridiculous from earlier sections, we can ask ourselves how far Gulliver now fits this idea. What is most ridiculous in his behavior? Is it not in his ways of looking at things? If it is enlarging and humanizing to see things in new and strange ways, what went wrong with Gulliver's learning? Acquiring a new way of looking at things should not mean losing touch with what one knows already. Our surrender should not be so complete. In order to grow, we must become the others we discover, but we can do so only to a point. When the awakening has been accomplished, it is necessary to go home again. The lesson looks ahead to our third text.

V

For a beginning pedagogy of *The Tempest* let me simply identify the main questions:

Are happenings in Prospero's island unusually strange or beyond belief as we compare them with happenings in "The Mariner" and Gulliver?

Gonzalo (V.i. 104–6) sums up the feeling of many: "All torment, trouble, wonder, and amazement / Inhabits here." It is difficult to know *what* to believe, for everything is strange. The spectator is at once caught up in a storm where all must surely perish, only to discover that all is illusion. But if the storm is an illusion, the *experience* of the storm is not. This paradox, which carries throughout the play, is worth discussion. People learn from illusions; people really change in a place where nothing is real.

A hopeful note for the theatre, and for the classroom, too. The island is a classroom, and Prospero is the teacher as Torpedo Fish.

How shall we describe Prospero as a teacher?

He quickly gives us reason to doubt his pedagogy. In Milan, his dedication to bettering his mind "awakened an evil nature" in his brother. On the island, his efforts to teach Caliban have had equally negative effects: Caliban was given words to name his meanings and so "know" them (I.ii.355–8), and he used the acquisition as a power to curse. He is "unteachable"—in some respects. But Prospero's strategies as teacher may have changed. They now include at least one that seems wise. First, he times his instruction according to occasion, need, and the preparedness of his students: "Hear a little further, / And then I'll bring thee to the present business / Which now's upon's; without the which this story / Were most impertinent" (I.ii.135–8). Ferdinand and the others will not learn until they are ready to learn and be changed by the wonder of it.

How does Prospero differ from the play's other teacher?

Having watched Prospero in his first instruction, we encounter another teacher whose mode is quite different. Gonzalo instructs, whatever the time or situation, by abstract aphorism. His "students" Sebastian and Antonio simply ridicule all he says. (Are we using "ridiculous" here as we came to understand it in *Gulliver*?) Alonzo protests (II.i.106–7), "You cram these words into mine ears against / The stomach of my sense," and will not believe anything he says. The problem of belief in teaching and learning is raised in two extremes. Gonzalo's students believe nothing he says. Miranda and Ferdinand believe easily what their teacher chooses to show them.

What kinds of students are Miranda and Ferdinand?

Miranda is an unusual student. She learns by empathy. She has watched the wreck and suffered with those she saw suffer (I.ii.5–6). She surrenders herself utterly to the text, and while this is risky and ultimately insufficient, it is the right beginning.

She takes everything personally, we would say, but not selfishly or subjectively. The teaching-learning process in I.ii deserves close attention, contrasted as it is with the failures of teaching Caliban, and then paralleled with the first instruction (I.ii.424–5) of Ferdinand. For Miranda and Ferdinand, learning is tied to awakening (as for the Mariner and Gulliver, perhaps with different meanings). What awakens is a "nature," good and evil. The awakening of an evil nature begins in selfish power and negation; the awakening of a good nature begins in wonder and amazement. So it is for Miranda throughout, to the climax of V.i: "Oh, wonder!" For Ferdinand it is similar. He is led by the strangeness of the music, hears Ariel singing of changes rich and strange, thinks with "O you wonder!" that Miranda is a spirit. Wonder and amazement pervade the experiences of the play. Is this wonder akin to the wonder of Gulliver or of the Mariner? How does it differ? How does this wonder lead to discovery and knowing?

Do the spirits of the island challenge our beliefs in the same ways?
In *Gulliver,* too, the wonderer supposes that the strange being must be a spirit or supernatural creature. The spirits that fill the Mariner's world belong to natural places and beings. How does an Ariel differ from the spirits of the Mariner? The Mariner's spirits embody mysterious natural laws of justice, punishments, penance. Even a skeptic might believe that such spirits as justice are real. But what would it take to believe in an Ariel? How would such belief alter one's sense of everything?

How are wonder and ridicule connected here? As in Gulliver?
Belief in spirits is dangerous in this world. Some people (even Ferdinand and Miranda) seem fooled as to what a spirit is. They are "enchanted" or "charmed"—two key terms of the play that must be understood. Belief is treated not just with wonder but sometimes with ridicule. For Trinculo, Caliban is a strange beast or monster that "makes a man" (II.ii.30–32). Stephano thinks Caliban and Trinculo devils. Caliban thinks both the others brave

gods, and he worships them. Caliban is a "most ridiculous monster" who makes "a wonder of a poor drunkard" (II.ii.168–70).
Wonder and the ridiculous come together; the line is thin—even
when Ferdinand and Miranda believe each other spirits. But it is
part of Prospero's plan that they think so at first, for love and
learning begin in wonder. People are what they believe, what
uses they make of their beliefs.

How are people's beliefs tested and changed? How about
ours?
People in the play are constantly having their beliefs tested. They
do not know quite what to believe or whether they are waking
or sleeping. Their sense of what is possible is being tried and
changed. If we are genuinely immersed in the play, then ours
may be as well. The chief cynic-villains of the play, Sebastian and
Antonio, are certain of what is possible and impossible. Then in
III.iii, their beliefs abruptly change. They are as absurd in their
belief as in their disbelief. The wise and kindly Gonzalo reminds
Alonzo that when they were boys they would not believe what
later they came to "know" (43–48). Events that seemed monstrous or "unnatural" must now be believed; however illusory,
they are true tests. If so, then the spectator too must be tested,
must have his beliefs challenged and enlarged, as the reader of
the "Mariner" and *Gulliver* must. This is learning to learn.

Prospero has played the Torpedo Fish effectively. Learning
demands wonder, immersion in discovery, and at times a be-
wilderment as to what to believe. True understanding requires a
shock of awakening to strange ways of viewing things. Following
such shocks and immersions, we can deal more effectively with
the Person from Porlock, his generic definitions, his rational categories, for we will have discovered where they come from, and
how and why to invent them.

FOUR

*Reinventing
the Wheelhorse*

I

The Person from Porlock is more likely to take
control in another kind of first course. The one we have just ex-
amined is exploratory, predisciplinary, even though it can make
its own moves toward precision and conceptual repertoire. Its
texts are literary, but its structures are philosophical. Literature
is the experience of ideas, a humanity. But what about the course
that introduces literature as an art? Which kind serves best in a
core curriculum? To decide, we would need to agree on the aims
of a core curriculum, and no faculty has ever quite managed to do
so. A few years ago, I chaired yet another committee charged to
make the attempt. Our history is revealing and poignant, but a
full retelling doesn't belong here. I must, however, summarize
our chief findings as a context for this chapter.

In the long and maculate history of general education, the
term "core" has had at least three meanings. First, once upon a
simpler time, it referred to a body of shared information and
privileged texts. Second, it referred to a structure of areas: humanities, natural sciences, social sciences, and so on. Third, it
evoked an idea both older and newer: a cluster of fundamental
disciplines that underlie all areas: inquiry, experiment, interpretation, argument, etc. These "core" ideas have been further
complicated by the growth of departmentalized "disciplines,"
whose introductory courses have often been confused with "core"
courses.

Our committee despaired of resurrecting the first idea. We were quixotic enough to combine the second and third ideas with the idea of the introductory major course. Our core courses would pursue three aims at once: (1) to provide a basic core of knowledge in a departmental "discipline"; (2) to introduce the general academic area which the discipline represents; (3) to provide training in some of the fundamental intellectual "skills" (the word provoked angry faculty debate). You will not be surprised to learn that the third aim dismayed many. Why should *they* teach writing and reading—even thinking? You may be surprised to learn that many could not understand the connection between the first two. Our challenge was bewildering. The mathematician Robert Gurland has described it best: "The challenge of college teaching consists of the concerted effort of every faculty member to reveal the organic relation between the material of his subject and the seminal concepts of both his discipline and others" (82). Even we teachers of literature, accustomed to our cross-disciplinary role, had some trouble with such a challenge.

Our committee had asked for trouble. Three of the general areas we defined were historical and cultural studies, humanistic-philosophical studies, and arts. Some introductory literature courses appeared in each of the three, calling for the introduction of literature in three different ways. There may be little general dispute about the classifications: literature is philosophical, historical, an art. The curricular issue is which ought to be emphasized first. The pedagogical problem is how to teach literature in *one* of these ways. The issue and the problem are aggravated by the fact of economic life in most universities and colleges. There simply isn't enough money, aren't enough faculty, to offer some courses for students in all fields and other courses for people beginning a major in literature. The same courses must double for both. But how can we design and teach a course that introduces, a course that prepares, when we don't know *who* is introduced, or prepared for *what?*

In chapter 3's course, the problem scarcely arises. But now we want to introduce literature as an "aesthetic object" and also as a "cultural-historical artifact." These are hard enough to coordinate, but when the problem of mixed clientele is added, the difficulties increase. I will assume the mixed clientele, and will suppose two courses to be taken in sequence (which first?): I. Literature and the Reader; II. Writers and Their Worlds. This chapter examines the first, and in it we will seek appropriate disciplinary strategies for the teacher as Person from Porlock.

Surveyed on their priorities for a preparatory course in literature, my well-meaning colleagues could agree on little. We agreed, you may recall, that literature must be taught historically. We also agreed that a first course should emphasize reading—reading closely, reading better. The consensus became misty when we tried to say what we meant. It was widely assumed that "learning to read better" is an isolable process, that it stresses "care" and "closeness," that it increases attentiveness; but what kind of attentiveness and attentiveness to what are not clear. One major pattern emerged: the attentiveness focuses on texts in themselves, not on associations, contexts, and motives. First we must teach "close reading." This consensus has a history, and the history is part of us.

We know that close reading was chiefly the bequest of the New Criticism of the forties and fifties, now remembered either as an embarrassing orthodoxy or as a stability before the flood. A cry of nostalgia for the blissful dawn of reading. A penny for the Old Guy. Now we feel defensive and the defensiveness confuses us; loyal and the loyalty divides us. Our disenchantment did not begin just the other day. How complacent I felt when Chicago's neo-Aristotelians labeled Cleanth Brooks a "critical monist" long ago! How exhilarating was my first reading of Northrop Frye's *Anatomy of Criticism* (1957) and Wayne Booth's *Rhetoric of Fiction* (1961), each with its pluralistic escape from that monism! Faithful to novels declared incoherent by Dorothy Van Ghent (1953), I had only to borrow a new combination label, and lo! the "bad novel" became a "romance-anatomy." We were entering upon the heady stage of multiplicity. We were becoming critical pluralists.

Many of us still are or want to think so. We are faithful to some "new critical *methods*"; we assume we can keep the methods without the approach. We call ourselves eclectics, sample new approaches, enlarge our repertoire, and teach something called a "total critical act." "Perhaps," writes Terry Eagleton,

> we should celebrate the plurality of critical methods, adopt a tolerantly ecumenical posture and rejoice in our freedom from the tyranny of any single procedure. Before we become too euphoric, however, we should notice that there are certain problems here, too. For one thing, not all of these methods are mutually compatible. (198)

Could he be right? Are the New Critical methods of close reading somehow incompatible with our new commitments? Eagleton interprets the phrase:

> To call for close reading, in fact, is to do more than insist on due attentiveness to the text. It inescapably suggests an attention to *this* rather than to something else: to the "words on the page" rather than to the context which produced and surrounds them. . . . [Close reading] encouraged the illusion that any piece of language, "literary" or not, can be adequately studied or even understood in isolation. . . . (44)

If we begin by teaching close reading, are we establishing this illusion that motive, context, and response are somehow independent of "understanding the work itself"? We want to teach a work as "aesthetic object" and later as "cultural artifact." But doesn't the very chronology make us prisoners of the illusion? And yet, how can we *not* do this when we want to cultivate a reverent attentiveness to the text itself? A key problem is in that loaded word "reverent."

Newer critics would displace close reading with a different idea of the total critical act, and they begin by attacking the attitude of reverence. Terence Hawkes supplies a useful summary of their assumptions [152–7]:

1. There exists no objective text to be revered, with its stored, fixed content, independent of author and reader;
2. There exists no such person as a reader who can confront directly the "words on the page" without personal and cultural lenses;

3. Writing and reading are not universal, "natural" processes;
4. No critical position is "neutral," that is, free of an ideology.

Some of us agree. Indeed, some of us will think the assumptions aren't so new as they are claimed to be. We came to them personally by various routes, and our personal histories can be illuminating.

My own suspicions arose when I was told that some of the works I valued most were unbalanced and incoherent. Were the "large, loose, baggy monsters" of nineteenth-century fiction really beyond the pale? Could *In Memoriam* not be powerful and inconsistent? I did not have to wait thirty years to hear from Eagleton that great literary works "may be diffuse, incomplete and internally contradictory," that there is no reason why an author "should not have had several mutually contradictory intentions" (74), that what is hidden or ambivalent in a work "may provide a central clue to its meanings" (178). Others may have come by other roads. Those who teach theatrical drama are accustomed to viewing the text of a play as a mere script. Those who teach autobiography cannot avoid texts that are "incomplete," texts whose blindspots and contradictory intentions are constitutive. They cannot teach an autobiography as an autonomous product; they must teach it as a process.

And there is a key to what was happening to us. By one route or another, we were struggling toward what Toby Fulwiler calls a "process orientation" in teaching and learning. Some of us acquired our process orientation through teaching composition. In the late 1950s, I was obliged to use textbooks that instructed a writer to formulate something called a "thesis" first, and then to outline a coherent paper to "carry out" that thesis. It did not take radical theory to discover that writing simply does not happen this way. An intention evolves as part of a process. Process was what we had to teach. About 1970, texts began appearing with titles like Young, Becker, and Pike's *Rhetoric: Discovery and Change*. The same year saw the appearance of Walter Slatoff's *With Respect to Readers*. For me, it was a momentous event—

texts are, after all, events. It told me I had become a teacher of the processes of reading literature. Knowing nothing yet of structuralist poetics, I was "granting new attention to the activity of reading," attempting to "specify how we go about making sense of texts" (Culler viii). Was I no longer teaching close reading?

In 1952, art historian Seymour Slive took a bunch of students to the Uffizi and pushed us physically to within ten inches of a painting. "Do you *see?*" he pleaded. I did not know what to see and saw only a blur, for myopia is not a normal way of seeing. We get closer to what we want to see not by shoving our eyes up to it, but by using a lens that focuses and magnifies, or a telescope that brings *it* closer to *us*. It took a while to learn to see a painting by what Wolfgang Iser calls "the wandering viewpoint," moving in and out, side to side, shifting position and focus. Why not a text as well? To "close reading" we might prefer "in and out and around reading." For many years, however, remembering Seymour Slive, I would command students to "look closely at the page in front of you." I felt irritated when instead they looked up in the air or out of the window. They were—some of them, at least—looking for that mental way into the text where alone the way could be found: in their minds. They were looking for their responses, but they were also looking for conceptual lenses, mental instruments. Preparatory teaching must provide such lenses and instruments, and it is the Porlockian task to provide them. But which ones, in what order, and how?

Students may indeed feel close to something they read, and then, when we push them into our kinds of attentiveness, they feel more distanced. They sense we are dissipating their closeness into analytical activities, dividing impressions into categories. Even a militant defender of "criticism" in literary education, James Gribble (*Literary Education: A Revaluation*, 1983), sees this as the basic problem:

> The most fundamental challenge to the literary critic is one which should be of great concern to the literature teacher— how to talk about *aspects* of works of literature without implying that the aspects are separable from the whole. How often, in classrooms, are students invited to subdivide their

account of the novel they have been reading under headings
such as "characterization," "description," "dialogue," "incident," "theme," etc. . . . I know from my own experience
how tempting it is to employ a simplified and compart-
mentalized critical vocabulary in teaching. . . . Both teachers and students have a natural preference for employing
terms in readily definable and categorical ways—it's easier to
learn these and thus easier to teach them. (44)

This is why introductory textbooks are in love with "elements." Even a text with a title I was drawn to, Leo Rockas's
Ways In (1984), falls into a lock-step design that moves from Formal Analysis through Rhetorical Analysis to seventy pages called
Analysis of Elements. These are not, for me anyway, Ways In. Of
course there are elements; the problem with the usual elements
is that they are not elemental. They are abstractions from whole
groups of elements. We cannot talk about a "plot" until we understand what an event is, what an action is, in what ways events can
be linked. We cannot speak of a "character" without understanding what we mean by role, motive, trait, and value. We cannot
make sense of "setting" without first clarifying time, location, and
circumstance. And as for "point of view": Is it a position in space,
in time, in ideology? A cluster of feelings and attitudes? A degree
of emotional or cognitive distance? How does it differ from "intention" and "theme"? Finally, the listing of style as an element
should remind us that whole books can be called "the elements of
style." Far from substituting elements of my own, I would urge
each of us to probe his or her own teaching to discover what fundamental dimensions of literary form and language *can* be learned
first, can best be grounded in the reading process, and can best
be used to generate a further recognition of "elements." If this
sounds like reinventing the wheel, it is.

II

In the simplest pedagogical terms, we can ap-
proach a literary text either as a verbal representation or as an

event, a happening. Approaching it as a happening may, at an introductory stage, be more immediately productive of active learning. The first question asked is not, "What is this about?" but
rather, "What happens here?" This is to bring directly into play
the unsophisticated reader in all of us, to appeal to the archaic
interest in "story." To ask, "What is this about?" is to force the
student into acts of referral, referring to constructs of reality, ab-
stracting something called a "subject." This is like seeking the
subject of a sentence before finding the verb. To ask, "What happens here?" is to begin with predication, with the making of
statements. Both questions call for interpretation, of course, but
interpretation of different kinds. "What happens?" calls for process analysis, shape-making, rather than substantive abstraction.

Once, in an introductory course, I asked students to read half
of Stevenson's *Kidnapped* and then provide written answers to
the question, "What happens in Lettermore Wood?" (chapter 7).
The answers were interpretive in various ways, on various levels
of abstraction, with various degrees of subjectivity. Some students reported matter-of-factly on external events, some identified changes of relationship, some identified variations of theme,
some described what happened *to* the *book* at this stage, some
described what happened to *them* as readers. Some answers
were selective and diagrammatic; sophisticated students came
with concepts fully formed. Others were relatively shapeless,
often more concrete and sensitive to detail. Some students focused on causes, some on effects, but most had difficulties setting
limits, saying where the happenings began and where they ended.
The idea of event or happening is so multifaceted as to make se-
lection and exclusion difficult. And this is its value as a starting
point. It opens in Whitehead's "romance." It uncovers many possibilities for making sense of a text. At the same time, it displays
for the teacher how his students read. The class can talk at once
about these possibilities and processes.

The follow-up to students' answers is not, "Is that correct? Is
it accurate?" but rather, "How did you arrive at that answer?"
This second question calls for the same kind of mental activity as
"What happens?" It asks for process analysis, and the answers

(inarticulate at first) direct our attention to the reading process. We try to articulate what happens in reading, become conscious of the processes of other readers, begin to look for the connections between what happens to us and what happens in the text.

This is only a first step. As we take it, we learn how stuck we are without a language to use in describing and explaining. We run up against our "cognitive incompetence," discover the only genuine motivation there is for learning: We learn what we need in order to know what we are learning and to learn more. What fundamental needs are likely to arise? I see three possibilities, and I will respond with three elements: *shape, impact,* and *reference.* When I ask, "What happens in Lettermore Wood?" the answers are struggles to describe something with shape, for without shaping there can be no answer at all. They are struggles to describe impact, for without impact there is no motive for answering. They are struggles to refer, for if the text did not remind the student of anything, however obliquely, he would have nothing to make an answer of. We discover these three fundamentals *together* from the very beginning. Each of them generates further fundamentals.

Shape leads to perceptions of structure, pattern. We try to identify parts, kinds of parts, kinds of connections among parts. We observe how works are given shape, how we shape them in memory, and how these two are never quite the same. I ask first, "What shape has this in your mind?" and afterwards, "How does your mental shape differ from the shape we seem to find on the pages?" Some things will have been forgotten, some added, some overemphasized and others slighted, some transposed or transformed. We study these "mistakes" experimentally, not to "correct" them but to understand how they happen. I am *not* suggesting that the only text that matters is the changeling in the reader's memory. There may be no one right response or real text, but we realize a limited number of coherent or valid responses when we check the text we are given.

Impact leads us to identify modes and intentions. We are affected not just in idiosyncratic individual ways, but in *kinds* of ways, and these kinds can be named: tragic, comic, realistic, fantastic, and so on. And when we are "impacted" by something another person has done or made, we ask why. This "why" is really two questions: (1) What causes are in me—are they mine alone? (2) What causes are in the maker?

Reference leads to discoveries of genres and expectations, of genres *as* expectations. We notice that certain works refer to the same kinds of things in similar proportions; we begin to compare them, classify them. We discover that we begin reading with certain general expectations of what the work will include, exclude, emphasize. Genre is not some absolute thing "out there"; it is real in us.

So where, in all of this, is the element called theme? How do we make our move to meaning? A theme is a motif that recurs in variation. What is a motif? Is any recurrent literary motif a theme: an occurrence, a situation, a kind of character or interaction, an image or phrase? If a literary work has as many themes as it has recurrent motifs, this does not bode well for finding *the* theme. Some would say that the theme is the "subject." But this may prove circular, for when asked what the subject is, they may have to reply, "the theme." Others would say, no, the theme is what the work "says about" the subject. It can only be formulated as a statement: love is a tyrant; war is hell; beauty lasts forever; history is a nightmare. But this is to equate theme with thesis. The term is more a nuisance than a help. I avoid it, and try instead to teach the kinds of mental acts we perform when trying to make sense of a shape. We observe recurrences. We classify those recurrences and so produce general ideas of what recurs. We observe recurrent connections, and if we can describe them together in a proposition, we have (whatever we call it) a theme. A theme is a statement by a reader; it includes a what and a why. It explains why things happen as they do to certain kinds of people in certain kinds of situations, and this explanation is the sense we make of the work's shape. This is where my naive question, "What happens in Lettermore Wood?" finally leads.

Some of us would begin instead by asking students to look closely at language. If we do not strengthen and cultivate language awareness, we are ignoring the most elemental element of all. But when we command, "Look closely at the language," do students already have the instruments to use? Which will we introduce? Introductory students begin to acquire the language awareness we hope for when they realize that words are *chosen* by someone, that other words might have been chosen. Hence the extraordinary pedagogical value of an author's working drafts and the usefulness of exercises in paraphrase: "Rewrite this passage using different words, and contrast the original to see what happens." And detection games: "Here are passages from our texts. Find all the verbal clues you can, clues to identity, to mood, situation, attitude." The discovery that words are clues to something called an "attitude" is the beginning of a new sensitivity to language's *expressive* aspect.

Another option is to begin with the *pragmatic* aspect. Words *do* something to a reader. A useful introductory exercise says, "After reading, pick the one passage that had the strongest impact on you. Try to figure out which choices of words had most to do with the impact. Describe as exactly as you can what happened to you." The discussion that follows should reveal that the causes of the impact are not simply "in the words." Where are they? They are contextual, and the contexts are dual. The reader brings contexts, but the text has created its own contexts, too, has connected words into recurrent patterns. The words come to us in patterns. We see them connect with each other. But where are these connections and how do we see them? The connections can be realized only in a reader's mind. So we might ask of a passage, a single phrase, a word, "What does it connect with in your mind? What does it *remind* you of? Does it lead you to remember another passage, phrase, or word from somewhere else? Memory works by connections. What's the connection?"

Different kinds of answers may be given. A student may be reminded of something outside the text, as well as something inside. The remembering that is essential to reading is often a fusion or *con*fusion of the two. One kind of remembering is not wrong or irrelevant; the kinds are different, and they function in different ways. Reading that treats the text as a closed system, an autonomous object, tries to deny the realities of the reading process.

If language expresses, impacts, connects, it also *refers*. Words evoke a picture of the world. The beginning student understands this representation according to how "familiar" it seems. The more familiar the words, the more of a "way in" he feels he has. But one of the essentials of literary language is that it defamiliarizes. And so, our leading question is not, "In what way do these words fit your habitual image of reality?" but instead, "What is most strange or unfamiliar about them?" An exercise might ask: "If you were to find yourself suddenly in the world these words create, what would be most strange?" Or specifically, "Which does the language make strangest: the world of Chaucer's pilgrimage? the world of Shakespeare's kings? the world of Milton's perfect beings? or the world of Austen's neighborhoods?" I hope that someone would choose Austen, for that would initiate a real howler of a discussion about what we mean by "realism"!

Such a howler raises our other problem as language teachers. At this Porlockian stage of precision, we feel obliged to insure that students acquire a literary or critical "terminology." Some of us even (I made the mistake once) order and assign a glossary of terms. Of course we need a terminology; without it, we cannot precisely share observations or responses, cannot precisely identify the features of texts that occasion them, cannot generalize about those features. The problem is when and how to get a terminology. In chapter 3, I described the process I believe in: discovering the need for a conceptual term (such as "genre" or "mode") and then inventing it. I would follow this process in the first course.

Our chief difficulties are two. First, students often bring with them a vague, misremembered, and inert terminology; making them unlearn it may be harder than teaching a new one. They can parrot the difference between metaphor and simile, the difference between iambic and trochaic, but cannot explain what they have in common, what metaphor or meter does. Second, they are all too ready to seize upon terms as absolutes and substitute them for understanding. Only as the need arises and provokes thought can words be truly learned. My basis here is Vygotsky's *Thought and Language:* "The relation of thought to word is not a thing but a process, a continual movement back and forth from thought to word and word to thought. . . . Every thought moves, grows, and develops, fulfills a function, solves a problem" (125). The point is not to teach a language, but to show how such a language is needed, created, and used.

To illustrate, let me recall two exercises from my own experimental teaching of a first course called Practical Criticism. The first writing exercise asked for responses to two short stories. Students were to answer one of five questions, and when we discussed their replies, we also analyzed why they had chosen the questions they chose: (1) Which relationship seems to you more believable, and why: Larry and his father in O'Connor, or Laura and Braggioni in Porter? (2) Which seems to you more necessary to the pattern of its story: Larry's "really nice model railway" or Laura's "flowering judas" tree? (3) Which situation seems more related to its story, and how so: World War I in Ireland, or the revolution in Mexico? (4) What is the main difference between the attitude toward sex and power you get from O'Connor's story, and the one you get from Porter's? (5) What differences might it make for you as reader if Laura told her own story, or if Larry's story were told by someone else?

As you might guess, questions one and four proved most popular. Students were eager to talk about "believability," relationship, and subject; but they lacked the language to do so with any precision. No one chose the "pattern" question, two; they were not ready to grope for descriptions of form, and no terminology would have helped them so early. Question three proved most tricky, for "situation" was hard to define, and formal relevance proved perplexing. What might be meant by "setting" was still to be explored. Number four drew the most engaged and thoughtful answers, and they led us to inquire how an attitude is identified. From here, we could move to meaning and viewpoint. Question five provoked a very few students into interesting speculations; these were the readers who already read with a writer's options in mind.

Overall, the discussions ran up against a "cognitive incompetence," a lack of precise and usable terms. In the classes that followed, with other texts, we sought out and experimented with terms to use. The midterm measured our progress:

1. Which of the following three happenings seems most important to the *plot* of its work: The death of Ikimefuna? The burning up of Bertha Mason? The buying of yellow shoes by everyone in Guellen?

2. Which of these three *characters* best exemplifies what the word *comic* means to you: Okonkwo's father? Brocklehurst? The Mayor of Guellen?

3. Which of the following happenings comes closest to your meaning for *realism:* Okonkwo's gun goes off and kills Ezeudo's son? Jane is summoned by Rochester's voice? Claire spends a million to have Alfred killed?

4. Which of these three events best illustrates what you take *allegory* to be: The killing of Alfred? The burning of Okonkwo's compound? The burning of Thornfield?

The results graphically illustrated the truth of Vygotsky's precept. Later, we discussed them. Obviously there were no single correct answers. We agreed easily, however, that some applications were more valid than others, some explanations more clear and coherent. We were making a common language to use.

I now begin advanced courses with an abbreviated version of this tactic. A first-day questionnaire (the course is the nineteenth-century novel) asks for students' working definitions of novel, realism, character, plot, and so on. The follow-up discussion sorts out and classifies the replies. Invariably we find that some students define "character" as individual representation, some as social role, some as plot function, some as theme variation. Some define "realistic" in terms of texture (vivid, immediate), some in terms of motivation (probable, believable), some in terms of attitude (realistic, nonidealistic). We agree on these several meanings, and proceed with a common terminology.

III

This wheelhorse disciplinary course, this Porlockian venture, works chiefly as a laboratory for defining responses, making sense of those responses, and finding precise terms to use in defining and validating them. We will ask the same questions again and again: What happens here? What kind of impact does it have on us? How is it shaped to cause that impact? How do the chosen words and word-patterns cause it? What is strange and new about its view of reality? We will, of course, introduce forms other than narrative (see chapters 7 and 8). But underlying all our questions is, "Why do people read literature anyway; what kinds of value do they receive?"

We have, remember, a mixed clientele; some value literature already, some do not. They need to be persuaded that literature is enjoyable, interesting, valuable, and the simplest rhetoric tells us we must show them that *we* find it so—indeed, that we can find *more* pleasure and value, and can help them do so. The primary goal of any first course is to strengthen and intensify the pleasure of reading, the motivation to read on. If we fail in this, nothing else matters. The goal is most likely to be won through a new sense of possibilities, a new confidence in response. Many beginners do not know that they have responses—valid ones, at least. The goal is blocked by premature technicality, by rigid insistence on validation, by excessive labeling, by presenting texts as examples of critical concepts.

But once we have brought students to (or near) this stage of confident enthusiasm, we must be ready to challenge it, to help them discover how much they do not know, discover that validity of response depends in part on other things, contexts. We must move them toward a new and more active reverence for the text as the work of an other—another person, another time, another culture. The next step—in whatever kind of course—is to study literature and the others.

FIVE

Literature and Others

We literarians claim to know that a "literary work is ineluctably a historical fact" and that we are all "creatures of the historical sense" (Trilling 181–3). We know that "literature confronts us both as social institution and as work of art" (Barthes in Burns 191). But many of us are not sure what, as teachers, to do about it. First we might follow the counsel of David Spring, a social historian who has "remained unrepentantly a believer in the utility of students of literature and students of history talking to one another more often than they do" (54). What might they learn from each other?

For starters, we could remind the historian that history is a kind of discourse, that any "event" can be known only as it becomes a text. They could remind us that any "text" is an event: it happened in certain circumstances. Thinking about every event as a text, every text as an event, we recall what an academic discipline really is: not a body of knowledge, but a way of thinking and speaking about all phenomena. Learning that a discipline is really a perspective on the world may be the most important (and difficult) aim of college learning.

In chapter 4, we considered one bequest of our new critical heritage: the narrowness of a close reading that excludes context. Another is a narrower definition of literature, a fairly recent one; in the eighteenth and nineteenth centuries, a broader view prevailed. Literature included "the whole body of valued writing in

75

society: philosophy, history, essays and letters, as well as poems"
(Eagleton 17). Our narrowness may well contribute to our difficulties in teaching literature historically and culturally, since it
stresses the special qualities of a literary text. In some parts of
this book, we must emphasize those special qualities. Here, we
focus on what texts of all kinds share.

Our students can (and must) learn that any text has been
made, has gone through the process of making, by an other, an
author. They also must learn that when we read we make our own
text of the one given us. Understanding is the process of interaction between reader and other, between author's making and our
remaking. From these two discoveries, a third can follow: reader
and other carry on their making in different circumstances, different contexts, and these contexts are a condition of understanding.
The contextual teaching of literature begins with two aims: (1) to
show students that texts are made by other persons in their own
circumstances, with their own perspectives and methods; (2) to
show students that, while they must recognize that other in the
text, they also compose their own text in their own contexts. Literary response in them, as in anyone, is historical and cultural.
We teach the contextuality of making and response.

To suggest ways of doing so, I want to consider texts of various kinds, and as a result, my examples must be numerous. We
will assume that the students addressed here have already passed
through their introductory encounters with the Torpedo Fish
and the Person from Porlock, and that the teacher has added a
third, somewhat different, persona to the repertoire. She is now
also a Guide to Context—biographical, historical, cultural. The
Guide's chief aim, and her problem, is to provide access to contextual information and to show when, how, and why it needs to
be used.

I

For me, the most useful kind of text to begin
with is biography. Few students are likely to become poets, novelists, historians, or social scientists; they are all, from time to

time, biographers—interpreters of the lives of others. Biography can turn up anywhere in the curriculum. It poses most directly the problems of knowing an other and an other's text. Here, then, are three examples from my teaching of biography. The point of the first, from Hellman's *Pentimento*, is to teach how we compose our own texts in reading; of the second, from Roper's *Life of More*, to teach that an episode has been circumstantially made; of the third, from Boswell's *Johnson*, to combine the first two discoveries.

My assignment was to read Hellman's separate sketches of Bethe, Willy, and Julia, and to discuss ways of grouping them. How we group (and how Hellman declines to group) the three persons affects how we know them. Knowing is forming. We can teach biographical form in two ways: take the form as a given and try to understand it; or take the particulars, try out our own ways of putting them together, and then compare our ways with the author's. Choosing the second, we approximate what the biographer had to do in what we do ourselves. The assignment went as follows.

Hellman's adolescence was marked by four or five memorable events. At about twelve, she spent a New Year's Eve with her "beloved friend" Julia at the grandparents' mansion, and at about sixteen she went with Julia and grandparents to the Adirondacks. About three or four years before college, Hellman went on a trip with Willy to the Cajun camp, and felt a turbulent mixture of emotions. During the same years, she visited Bethe several times. Suppose now, as Hellman's biographers, we try to fit them together and come up with some tentative ideas about this formative stage in her life, about her personality, her relationships, her sense of society.

1. What biographical importance do the episodes have singly and together? What revelations do they make?
2. We usually read biography forwards, but biography is created backward; from the present, the past is reconstructed. How might you relate these early episodes to major features of Hellman's later life: her relationship with Hammett; her vocation as writer; her politics?

3. As we give meaning to these episodes, we should also be aware of what meanings Hellman gives them, note the differences, and try to account for them. The meanings Hellman gives to her remembered experiences tell us about her. Memory, after all, is a personal thing. Andre Malraux once said that men [and women] "are distinguishable as much by the forms their memories take as by their character" (102). Are there any peculiarities in the ways Hellman's memory works (or doesn't work)?

4. We are ready to think about composing. If you were trying to organize these episodes into a single chapter of biography, in what order would you place them? How would you explain their connections? How might you frame them in place and time? Make up an opening paragraph.

Unfortunately I did not tape this class, and so I cannot "remember" the script of our discussion. It would be interesting to try reconstructing now, two years later, in the context of writing this book. I would surely come up with what Hellman calls *pentimento*. The result would be memory, but more. It would be, in Aristotle's distinction, an act of recollection. It is an art, and since we all practice it, we are all biographers. We practice it in our own circumstances.

The second episode is a piece of William Roper's Tudor gem, his memoir of his father-in-law. It recounts Thomas More's final departure from home on the day he is summoned to the commission that will send him to prison and the headman's block. The incident happened, we know, in 1534, and Roper wrote the episode, we also know, twenty years later. It is often cited as a prime example of Roper's "art." If we take the episode as narrative art, we see that it centers on the major character at a climactic point in a story. We notice its narrative structure, language, point of view. We seek meaningful patterns (themes) and make judgments. We do what we do with any invented narrative.

But a phantom haunts us, and the phantom is reality. In fiction, the narrative episode *is* the reality. In biography, it is only the shadow of a reality that has been processed. Somewhere, somewhen, were the perceived facts of More's behavior, and Roper was the one who perceived them. At some point, perhaps then, perhaps later, Roper perceived them in the light of what he had conceived of as More's "accustomed manner," and perceived them as unusual. Twenty years later, Roper recollected and composed the episode in light of later circumstances that made it safe and desirable to tell More's story sympathetically. "It" became an exemplum and a portent, a pictorial emblem and a proleptic symbol of More's personality and fate. At some point in this process Roper linked the "it" of the wicket gate with the "it" of the dialogue in the boat, which he did not understand at the time, but understood by *conjecture* afterwards. By recollecting, he made sense of "it." Composing his memoir, he selected "it" as *memorable*—not just remembered but worthy of memory—and worked it into his pattern of anecdotes. He made it in his own later circumstances.

Which "it" are we speaking of? Where, in this process, does "it" acquire its meaning and its form? Whatever the answers—if we could ever find them—one thing is apparent. In seeking the meaning of a biographical episode, we readers are always driven to ask questions about the process by which it came into being as a text. The biographer and his process move into our consciousness. The more they do so, the more we ourselves actively associate with the biographer and his process.

The third episode is the famous Wilkes dinner in Boswell's *Johnson*. It serves us well, first, because Boswell shows so openly how he made it, and, second, because we are so tempted—like any other biographer of Johnson—to remake it into something different. We can reconstruct Boswell's assumptions about art and psychology, and place them in historical context; we can see how influenced he was by his immediate audience's expectations. The episode "must, by anybody's reckoning, rank among Boswell's finest performances" (Siebenschuh 98), and the word "performance" is noteworthy. The text is Boswell's *performance*—this is what we want to emphasize. Besides, Boswell always performed so as to make life into a text.

His art is often discussed: the methods he uses to draw the reader into the scene and to manipulate matter and reader toward certain aesthetic ends. Fine, so long as we also discuss our distance, or resistance. As we watch and admire his making of his text, we must also make our own. What must a reader feel and think when Boswell exults at getting Johnson into the coach like an heiress carried off to Gretna-Green? Or when he declares that, having trapped Johnson into this awkward situation, Boswell "kept myself snug and silent, watching how [Johnson] would conduct himself"? Or when he leaps from cautious inference to the omniscient assertion that Johnson "resolutely set himself to behave quite as an easy man of the world, who could adapt himself at once to the disposition and manner of those whom he might chance to meet"? Who actually succeeds at such adaptation in Boswell's stage-managed episode? It is surely not Johnson, but Wilkes. It is Boswell himself who has to save the day. We may be struck by how easily this Johnson of extraordinary intellectual powers could be flattered and fooled, hardly supportive of the admiration for Johnson that Boswell seeks (he says) to arouse. Or maybe we ask, "Why did Johnson put up with such treatment?" Increasingly, we find our attention to Johnson deflected by our preoccupation with the Johnson-Boswell relationship. This relationship is a condition of our understanding.

The point is not to prove Boswell wrong. The point is simply to illustrate that Boswell is the maker (in more ways than one) of the episode. But what we remake of it may be far from what Boswell makes of it. Our perspectives as readers are bound to differ. We should contrast some of the ways modern biographers understand (that is, remake) Boswell's episode differently. Wain sees it as exemplifying a time when Johnson's life as a social lion reached its peak, and when his enjoyment of a few good late years brought out his more charitable and compassionate side (342). Bate places it in Johnson's "Indian Summer," a period when, aware of growing infirmities, Johnson made a special effort to acquire "good humour," "easiness of approach," "softness of manner" (510). Such interpretations are certainly challengeable, like all biographical interpretations, but they must be made.

And two points ought to be made about this teaching. First, expect students to be unnerved. The generic norms they bring with them are violated by such uncertainties. In fiction, they expect an author whose subjective vision, however eccentric or distorted, is legitimate. In biography, or history, they expect the opposite. The givens of fiction are invented; the givens of biography or history are "known." The naive reader begins in the absolutist assumption that biographer, historian, or social scientist is a truth-teller or nothing. Moving to multiplicity or romance, the student discovers that the biographer's is only one partial, subjective impression of the truth. The move to precision stresses a more disciplined understanding of how, within what circumstances, and from what historical perspective the biographer made her biography. The outcome ought to be the realization of context.

Second, we all read such "non-literary" texts differently at first. We expect to look at a "literary" text in and for itself; another kind is a text *about* someone or something. It refers to a subject, a body of knowledge. This other text is merely a medium. What must be learned (however painfully) is that the distinction isn't so simple, that this other text too has been made by an other; we are forced back upon the process of its making, and upon the realization that the process was circumstantial. The relationship of biographer to subject is the context of reading any biography. The relationship of author to subject, like that of reader to subject, is a historical-cultural phenomenon. The same is true of any kind of text.

II

This is not meant to break down all generic distinctions in our teaching. Part of the value of Hayden White's essay "The Historical Text as Literary Artifact" is that it insists on some distinctions. It does not simply argue that historical texts are translations of "fact" into "fiction." It does explain that historians are influenced by literary models in making sense (and form) of their materials. It helps us teach that (as Murray Krieger says) a history has "its patterned reductions, its interpretive consistency" (68)—or perhaps inconsistency—its "intellectual form which provides the tune to which the sequence marches" (52). Coherence is achieved (as White says) more by what is left out than by what is put in, by suppression or subordination of certain elements, by "characterization, motific repetition, variation of tone and point of view, alternative descriptive strategies, and the like" (47). Information is placed in sets of relations, in forms "not immanent in the events themselves." They exist in the mind of the author and reflect "the myths, fables, folklore, the scientific knowledge, religion, and literary art" of his culture (55). Like any text, this one has been produced, even though its "mode of production" may be concealed:

> The language . . . may impress or intimidate us because we do not see how the language got there in the first place. The text does not allow the reader to see how the facts it contains were selected, what was excluded, why these facts were organized in this particular way, what assumptions governed this process, what forms of work went into the making of the text, and how all of this might have been different. (Eagleton 170)

If we teach historical or scientific texts, we can ask "detective" questions, such as: What kinds of facts are we given? What kinds do we miss? What organizing patterns can we identify? What kinds of language are we aware of? What attitudes or points of view reveal the author's kind of interest? How *might* "all of this have been different"? We can do a little of what goes at present under the intimidating label of *deconstruction*. But our usual concern as literarians is with the other side of the coin. How can we teach a literary text not as an "aesthetic object" with its all-sufficient self-referential economy, but as an event reflective of its historical and social contexts? Let me recall an example from the teaching of fiction.

Some years ago, in a team-taught interdisciplinary course titled Authority, Liberty, and the Law, my colleague, a political scientist, and I built our syllabus in three historical units. In each unit, we paired a novel with a work of social history. Our eighteenth-century unit paired Fielding's *Joseph Andrews* with a modern historical analysis (by Douglas Hay) of changing ideas of property and legal authority. My colleague reacted as many teachers do when on holiday from normal disciplinary pursuits. He enjoyed fiction, and when he led our initial discussions, he approached the novel as a "literary text" to be read as a self-contained fiction. It then became my job as Guide to provide historical context. To do so, I first constructed my own historical text, a vignette of the changing world of Fielding, and offered it as a lecture. As I went along, we considered what new dimensions of understanding certain episodes and relationships we might gain from placing our two texts together. Here are the opening passages of my counter-text.

As we have noticed, most of *Joseph Andrews* takes place on the road—the dirt, unleveled road between London and Somerset, between city and country, more than two centuries ago. Look at a map of England and find London at the southeast corner. Let your eye travel west to the Bristol Channel, drop an inch, and you will find the county of Somerset. Color Somerset green, and check the scale of miles: about 100 miles from London, two hours by motorway, like driving from Boston to Amherst. We have seen how slow and dangerous a trip this was then, how many confusing inns, rough rides, slow walks, dangerous encounters. Now you can begin to realize what local authority meant, how remote London seemed, how slowly things changed.

Living in this world, you scarcely notice that change is accelerating. Traditions of local authority are crumbling, the powers of central government growing. Shortly, as we have learned from Hay's essay, a local landowner can get a "law" passed in faroff London "authorizing" him to enclose local lands, fence them off (did you notice fences in the novel and how they functioned?), lands that have been "common" for generations. If you go onto his lands, you invade his "privacy," his "property." Why would he do this? Land is more valuable, worth more "money." Strange new connections, these. Why is land worth more? Scientific agriculture is beginning. Populations are growing, food supplies must grow, land must be "productive." All this sounds familiar in 1988, but with Fielding we are back at the beginning.

There may be another explanation for enclosing. Local landed aristocrats are under pressure from new families. They don't want their hunting—aristocratic pastime—interfered with. A new idea of social control is to keep others out, be exclusive. And when this doesn't work, they will need new forms of enclosure to keep undesirables in, new institutions: criminal enclosures called prisons, madhouses called asylums, poor farms called workhouses (hard to distinguish from workplaces called factories). New centralized institutions such as these reflect a new idea of social control.

In a time when traditional authorities are breaking down— local, domestic—and when the church is weaker, when there is no modern police force, what sort of social control can we use to keep the fabric of authority together? The answer was, a system of laws, an institution of The Law, that terrified people by its majesty. (Hay makes us see how powerfully aesthetic an institution the law seemed. The law uses aesthetic devices all the time. Can you think of modern illustrations?) Fielding himself was a lawyer, a justice of the peace, and his novel has lots of both. Why does he seem so critical of them? What gives them such power in this social world, and in what ways do they misuse their authority, misuse the law as a form of social control? Do you find other persons misusing authority in the public world of this novel?

Fielding was an aristocrat as well, and he had little use for a new middle-class morality that was assuming social power. This new morality linked property with sex, and he attacked it as an aristocrat with strong sympathies for the poor, with a belief that all "classes" (the word wasn't invented yet) share the same passions and foibles, however they try to hide them. He attacked with a comedy of exposure. (His favorite episodes of exposure take place in coaches and inns. Why do such settings serve him so well? Would a modern novelist find the same use in trains and motels?) The technique of exposure has a long literary tradition, but Fielding uses it to portray the breakdowns (as he saw them) of social authority in his world. Let's consider chapter 12 (the coach scene) and the episode that follows at the Tow-wouse Inn. What connections are made between sex and property? Where else have we seen the same connections? [Discussion.]

How about the novel's domestic world? Joseph is a servant under the power or authority of his mistress and the upper servants. This system was taken for granted in Fielding's world. What disturbs Fielding is not the system but its misuse. Lady Booby supposedly wields authority over her household. Why is it that she cannot govern her own household? What power of social control rules Lady Booby, making her, she says, a "slave"? (We are familiar still with the word "fashion," but what meaning and force did it have in Fielding's world?) Compare Lady Booby's misuses of authority with those of Mrs. Slipslop and Mrs. Tow-wouse, and with those of the justices and lawyers.

The central relationship of the novel, we have seen, is between the servant Joseph and the local Anglican priest Parson Adams. (Can we really understand this relationship out of historical context?) We follow Joseph's struggles with the need and the natural impulse for "deference." (Do we still have this word?) Adams is a figure of traditional authority, and yet he is a poor guide. Why is his authority so often ineffectual? Are the causes of breakdown in authority part of him or part of his world?

The author does not present Adams as a perfect being; the book portrays no perfections because the author knew that his own authority (the two words are obviously related!) would be weakened if he did. The ways an author wields control over his text reflect his idea of what authority should be, and Fielding's is an eighteenth-century idea. Find some illustrations of how Fielding uses his authority. What qualities make him authoritative? Is he similar to, or different from, Adams?

And so on. So goes my attempt at context-building. My last question introduces the author as ultimately the central character in his text, but also as the historic personage whose authority makes this text. I am trying to make the transition back from the historic personage to the artist and to the book as a controlled design, while at the same time suggesting that this design can be understood only by reference to Fielding's world and his ideas about how it is designed. My way is lined with traps. The chief trap to avoid is the assumption that Fielding's fictional history— or any other history—can be taken simply as a record of the "real England" in which he lived. Somehow my students must be guided past Scylla and Charybdis: on one side, the assumption that fiction can be read as history; on the other, the assumption that the line between them is sharp and stable.

My own good guide here is the social historian David Spring. Discussing a slightly later novelist, and recalling Trilling's thesis that Jane Austen's *Emma* has little if anything to do with "the real England," Spring wonders how any serious historian would understand that term "the real England." Which "real England"? he asks. His answer is at once more historical and more literary than the "sort of bogus history" some literarians invent "when in need of historical background."

His approach to the historicity of Austen's novels is semantic. When historians "make sense" of a past, they are as dependent as we on language. The coinage of a term—he cites Everitt's "pseudo-gentry" (people competing to acquire the "trappings of gentry")—helps to make sense of Austen's world. Her own vocabulary does, too. As close readers, our students may be able to recognize that Austen's vocabulary is predominantly social. The term "neighborhood" is "one of the prime words in her social vocabulary." The "most cherished of social delights" (60) in that world is "privacy," and the "most desirable of all social states" is "independence." The institution of marriage plays a uniquely important role in making this social world and "confirming its arrangements" (61). We ask our students to compile such a lexicon, remembering that our meanings are not enough; that Austen, like all artists, defamiliarizes such familiar meanings, but that this defamiliarizing is not just aesthetic. It is also a consequence of our historic distance.

The art-critics of Austen have properly made much of Austen's ideal of working on "three or four families in a Country Village" as an aesthetic model. But her idea of "neighborhood"— with its cognates of simple elegance, "unpretending comfort," lack of clutter and noise, private spaces—is also a response to her perceived social world. What special, powerful meanings, did these terms have for her, and why might they have acquired such meaning and force in her historic world? Why, that is, did people like Austen (and Wordsworth, and shortly Mill and others) perceive society as having become oppressive, anonymous, inauthentic, repressive of individuality and independence? At the end of this chapter, I will address these questions to a Wordsworth sonnet. But first, there are other kinds of texts, other "others," to identify.

Teaching Fielding and Austen, it is the otherness of history that matters most. Some texts require us to teach the otherness of culture, for they are cross-cultural translations. In an introductory course called Law and Justice, I taught Achebe's novel *Things Fall Apart*, which portrays a traditional African village culture at the moment of conquest by European "civilization." Centering on the hero-deviant-scapegoat Okonkwo, the author reveals the culture's families, friendships, economies, rituals, and methods of social control. Achebe is an Ibo two generations removed, whose father was a Christian missionary, an Ibo who attended an African English university, studied European literature, used European literary models, and wrote about Ibo customs and values in English words. The book is a cultural translation. Achebe takes his title of cultural disintegration from a Yeats poem. In this and other ways he claims a universality of theme. The claim is a bit misleading. Here are a few of the questions we pursued:

1. So far, we have thought of law as a codified system of *statutes*. Anthropologists take a broader view of law as a set of *conventions* used by a society for social control. In

this sense, does Ibo society have laws? How does Ibo law differ in kind from our law?

2. In any novel, we can understand a theme only as it relates to other themes. For example, the Ibo have "property," and much of *our* law is based on property. But consider scenes where the Ibo talk together about ownership, debts and borrowings, wealth. Is their idea of property different from ours? Do they attach different kinds of value to property? (Consider yams!)

3. The word "justice" is often used in the book. But what is their idea of justice, and how do they feel about justice? Collect some instances. We hear talk of "just wars," the "justice" of the earth goddess, the just punishment of "crimes." How are their ideas of justice related to their ideas of crime and fairness?

4. They hold people responsible for their actions. They uphold rights and privileges according to status. Is their idea of responsibility different from ours? How are rights and privileges assigned? Are rights and responsibilities connected? What is their idea of status?

5. Here is an experiment. Suppose yourself an Ibo. A foreign British official comes to you and says, "This man Okonkwo is obviously a problem to your society. He beats up his wife, he kills a man; he profanes your rituals. Your system can't cope with this repeat offender. Your customs don't function as well as our laws." How will you defend your system?

6. Achebe wrote that his purpose was to teach foreigners something about his culture. He wrote, "African people did not hear of culture for the first time from Europeans; . . . their societies were not mindless but frequently had a philosophy of great depth and value and beauty . . . poetry, and, above all, they had dignity." Is Achebe using the word "culture" the same way we do? Can we measure its depth and beauty? Does what we call "art" have a function in this culture, and is the function the same in our culture?

III

    Literarians and historians sometimes misunderstand each other; literarians and social scientists make a habit of doing so. Our differences of perspective and method are, of course, radical; our kinships, often clouded, are more important. We literarians hope to teach literature as a social institution, institutions in literature, literature as a form of social understanding. But how can we do so without the aid of borrowed concepts and methods? How else can we employ what Lucien Goldmann calls the "historico-sociological method" in our teaching (109)?

    Our differences are not just verbal. The social scientist wants students to infer conceptual structures from the data of behavior. To this end, he "disambiguates" words, fixes their denotations, to make them "operational." To operationalize a "variable," he must do so. (Humanists often groan at such terms. Bear with me.) To operationalize a variable in a literary text is quite the opposite. The concept is made concrete; its ambiguities are exploited; its implications can be realized only in a texture. For the scientist, "What does A mean?" is an instrumental, analytic question: "How can I use it in a controlled inquiry?" For the literarian, "What does A mean?" is experiential, synthetic: "How does its meaning feel in a context of other felt meanings?" Fictional literature, writes Avrom Fleishman, "is the place where concepts and facts are allowed a moment of rest and contemplation in their own right, before continuing their energetic careers" (22).

    Struggling through such thickets, we may find kinships. Here is a definition: "An invented or imagined construct to use in making sense of or trying to explain the world or some portion of it." What have I defined? Some may answer, "Theory, Model"; others, "Myth, Fiction." All are right. Fleishman reminds us: "As in the human sciences, which have been shown to operate by conceptual schemes tantamount to fictions, the role of literary fictions is to locate us in our human world, to contrive for us a securer perch in reality by all the arts at its disposal" (13).

    The models social scientists make are useful fictions; the fictions literary artists make are useful models. The metaphors artists make are constructs of reality; the constructs of reality scientists make are metaphoric. What the scientist calls a hypothesis is a fantasy, an "as if" invention in words. What the artist calls a fantasy is a hypothesis. What the scientist calls correlation is close kin to what the artist calls form. Both study variables in search of laws, though one may call these laws rhythms or patterns. Reality is a construction, not a given; realisms are made, not born. The sociologist Robert Nisbet sums up: "The science of sociology makes its most significant intellectual advances under the spur of stimuli and through processes that it largely shares with art; . . . whatever the differences between science and art, it is what they have in common that matters most" (477).

Using one text, let me suggest two applications to our teaching. First, we "read" the text, read in it what Trilling calls a culture's "hum and buzz of implication." Second, we study responses *to* the text. The actual course recalled here, Life Cycles, was an interdisciplinary introduction to sociology. The text, Sherwood Anderson's *Winesburg, Ohio,* portrays in interconnected short stories persons of the town, most of them haunted by a sense of failure and loneliness. The young hero is seen growing up into the work of a writer. Work as an institution is our subject. We try to understand work in Winesburg, and to correlate work with feelings of success and failure. Surely this effort is a legitimate *part* of a literary reading. Are the ways we do it fundamentally different from the scientist's ways?

If, as Kenneth Hoover argues, scientific method is simply a refinement of the systematic thinking we try to do all the time, why should they be? We are trying to make sense of stories with connected "themes" (variables) of work, success, happiness. We qualify the variables; we also quantify them: is A happier or more successful than B? We measure on some scale. Anderson shows us a social situation with a measurable lack of happiness and success, and imagines a hypothesis of why. We formulate hypotheses of his hypothesis and try them out. What is a hypothesis, and how (if not by the imagination) is it invented? (Every introductory science course must address such questions.) A hypothesis is a statement that proposes a correlation between certain variables. A hypothesis, says Hoover (84), is an *imagined* relationship that is then "put to the test."

We try out the variables in possible relations: upon what qualities of work does happiness or success depend? We examine the evidence to make sure we are looking at real instances of happiness or success ("real" as the context appears to define them), and note how frequently they occur together, and in correlation with what qualities of work. Alice Hindman, Wash Williams, Enoch Robinson, Elmer Cowley, Ray Pearson—all seem studies in failure. They are plain and dull; their lives are narrow and monotonous; their jobs are boring routines; some are lonely, don't trust others, have trouble communicating. What elements of failure do they share?

Let's hypothesize (suppose "as if") that failure has a lot to do with work in this culture. What is special about the ways these people work and about their feelings and attitudes to their work? Perhaps if we compare them, arrange them on a scale, putting "success" at one end and "failure" at the other, we can begin to see how work and success are correlated. At one end, Joe Welling seems relatively successful. What is his job role? How is it related to his other roles, to his needs and values? At the other end, Alice Hindman seems extremely unsuccessful and unhappy. How much does her sense of failure have to do with her job? We could choose the farmhand, Ray Pearson, worn out and resentful, or the merchant Ebenezer Cowley, "not happily placed" in his work. Who goes nearer the positive end? Enoch Robinson is "happy" with his job; Wash Williams is proud of his work, thinks of nothing else. Half-witted Turk Smollett sees work as his only badge of status; he "belongs" as the berry-pickers belong. We glimpse a pattern, a hypothesis: perhaps success depends on how one uses work: for some, work is personal identity; for others, work is a hiding place. Joe Welling stands out clearly now. He is happy with his work, yet he lives creatively in other roles, and maintains his personal passion for ideas.

We understand our scale better, our variables better, and we are clearer as to what our text means.

What it means to *us*—what it "signifies"—may be somewhat

different. The social situation out of which Anderson made the book, and the society it portrays, both seem remote. To under-stand—not the book itself, but our responses to it—we need to understand ourselves as readers. The understanding of literary response is another legitimate aim of literary study; just as surely, literary response is in part a function of social history and must be studied accordingly. Our class will design and conduct a survey of ourselves as readers, and tabulate and discuss the results. (1) How much (scale of 1 to 4) did you enjoy *Winesburg, Ohio?* How much (same scale) did it interest you? (2) What kind of reading do you like most (a list of choices)? (3) What do you value most in and about a work of fiction (a list of choices)? (4) How would you iden-tify yourself in terms of age group, gender, kind of employment or vocation, ethnic background, politics, religion? Putting our re-sults together, what hypotheses can we come up with to explain why certain people respond positively to the book, and others do not? Making sense of how people respond will help us under-stand better the social-historical institution called literature.

IV

My examples have been taken from narrative fiction, perhaps the easiest form to study contextually. Let me close with a very different kind of example. About 1807, Words-worth began a sonnet:

> The world is too much with us. Late and soon,
> Getting and spending, we lay waste our powers;
> Little we see in nature that is ours.
> We have given our hearts away, a sordid boon.

Teaching this sonnet, the Torpedo Fish might begin with a ro-mance exploration of what kind of experience is being conveyed here, what situation seems to be arousing such a hostile response, whether we recall having like experiences with like effects. The Person from Porlock might enter, then, and carry on a disciplined examination of the poem's shapes and linguistic strategies, a close reading. There would still remain important questions that had not been answered, questions of historical semantics and reference. *What* "world" is "with" this speaker? Why are "we" passive while the world is threateningly active? What "getting and spending" fill our time, and how is it that these economies produce only waste? Can we really guess or infer what kind of "power" he feels is wasted and what sort of "nature" seems opposed to this world, and why does he connect "see" with "heart"? We sense meanings we cannot grasp. What features of the world Wordsworth perceived about 1807 might help explain this response, and how might his response guide us to a better sense of that world?

Fragmentary footnotes and isolated explications won't give the answers. The teacher as contextual guide will need to provide a brief, coherent, and imaginative text—an image of the "world" Wordsworth believed he saw. We cannot grasp his act of perception without some effort to recreate its object. Certain information is needed, and no habit of disparaging "informative" teaching must prevent giving it. It needn't be dense, and it certainly should not be inert. It might follow (and flesh out) such general lines as these.

His "world" is a place of accelerating and oppressive social and economic change. The sense of space has changed: cities and towns are exploding in density; revolutions in communication and transport have made the world seem suddenly closer, "too much with us." Time has changed, too—"late and soon." The "world" has become obsessed with "getting and spending"—banks, credit, paper money, what Coleridge calls "the commercial spirit." Rural life is dominated by the "world" of urban fashion, and "nature" is being dispossessed or "improved" by entrepreneurs. A world of distracting spectacles is displacing the traditional insights of "the heart."

Now, any such reconstruction is not to be presented as a "background" to Wordsworth's poem. Even if I believed that some such historical situation in some respects "caused" Wordsworth's poem, I would not follow a cause-effect order in teaching. The effect of opening with the old "background introduction" and then shoving the poem in front is the effect of some Victorian novelists—say, Hardy—who create an overwhelming image of the landscape, and then against that huge backdrop place the small, isolated human figure. The effect is not to show how the figure, the text, is part of the context, but how remote and alienated it is. Rather, we need first to focus on an image of the figure or text—however mysterious in its possibilities (Whitehead's first stage)—and then identify and construct the peculiar features that provide a context, a context seen through the text. (The "hermeneutic circle" is a fair game in pedagogy.)

This is not to imply that Wordsworth's view of "the world" of 1807 is accurate, or historically legitimate. It simply suggests that such a powerful response was one way of "making sense" of that world and that this historical world can be better recovered and understood if we see how such sense-making went on.

What kind of a "historical explanation" of Wordsworth's poetic response do we offer? The danger is in going to one extreme or another. We might offer merely "factual" information, which is hard to convert to an understandable frame of mind or state of historic consciousness. Or we might conceptualize too much. We do not want to say, "Wordsworth responded this way to the perceived world of 1807 *because* in 1803–1806 Public Events A, B, and C took place." Nor do we want to say, "Wordsworth responded this way *because* he was a convert to Burkean conservatism, was a primitivist, an organic pastoralist, an anti-utilitarian." Most people do not perceive the world they live in as news chronicle or ideological construct. Neither will offer access to the historic experience of living according to certain values in certain circumstances.

We need both fact and idea, image and concept, and the kind of language that brings them together is metaphor or figure. Major shifts in historic experience are marked, we have often been told, by shifts in figurative ways of seeing the world. Perceiving an epoch as a figurative way of seeing the world, and historic change as a dialectic of successive metaphors, will surely not satisfy any historian—nor should it. But it is a graphic start. To view history through such awareness is a beginning in the pedagogical economy. Used carefully, it reveals what institutional tensions and transitions marked the period, how they shaped the contemporary consciousness of instability, of confrontation between old and new, of divided affiliations, of revival and renewal. And having at least recognized what these were, we can return to the text as an act, an event, of sense-making.

SIX

Art in History; or, Can Surveys Live?

I

For many of us, the contextual teaching of literature is not done in the experimental interdisciplinary situations I have been recalling. It is done, rather, in our old curricular catchalls, the period surveys. Catalog listings still abound. Teachers often take them as mere umbrellas under which various pedagogies can find shelter. But no kind of course makes heavier pedagogical demands. No kind seems better suited to the final stages of a student's program and development—from a first predisciplinary awakening to literary possibilities, through precise study of forms and kinds, through the discovery of *how* an art work is also an artifact, to a synthesis of modes in a certain epoch. This chapter might better come last, but its argument can best be understood as an extension of Literature and Others.

Can the survey live? It is impossible, we think, to teach a real survey course, but some of us feel we must keep on trying. Is it merely the conservative side of us, the nostalgia for some past wholeness? You can spot a traditionalist curriculum by a predominance of period surveys, and a traditionalist core by its requirement of British Literature I and II; American Literature I and II. The people who may become teachers must be "exposed" to the major periods, and so we must "cover" them. In turn, these teachers will perpetuate the survey as high-school literature courses (no more of that 1960s jazz, please!), which in turn will perpetuate our need to prepare them for it. Nowhere do our stubborn (dead) metaphors of exposure and coverage hang on more doggedly. As usual, the terms we use bury or beg fundamental questions. As usual, their unpacking will help us to a better understanding and thence to better designs and pedagogies. The survey can indeed live and even flourish, but only if we understand what it can be.

Our survey problem is the same nagging anxiety we feel about the scope and shape of any course, in a more extreme form: the despair that we cannot begin to cover what we take to be our subject, aggravated by a suspicion that students nowadays come to us having read less, and that we must compensate. The more we compromise our expectations, the guiltier or more frustrated we feel. The suspicions were voiced during my distant undergraduate days, and no doubt late Victorians heard the same lamentations. The survey must survive. We yearn to preserve such courses out of dismay at students' disinterest in literary pasts, and serious students share or acquire our guilt feelings about "gaps." What blushing gap confessions I have heard in my office. It is unclear whether this gap-complex has to do with history, or with the neglect of classics, or with an ignorance of literary diversity. It would help to decide.

If diversity is what we want to be learned, then we should design accordingly. If our goal is the study of literature in cultural contexts, then contextualism should guide us, and contexts are not just historical. If familiarity with a canon of classics (received or revisionary) is what matters, then diversity and contextualism may be misleading guides. Works do not become classic by dint of diversity, and the received idea of the classic is anticontextual: it is timeless, universal.

What do we mean by *survey* anyway? To survey a field—a spatial metaphor, not a temporal one—is to fix its boundaries and contours, to draw the configurations of its landmarks. Surveying is a mapping enterprise, and a map, Robert Harbison tells us, is a mental miniature, an artifice of the mind. There are many kinds of maps, and we must choose before making one. A map, however artificial, is an extremely useful heuristic device, created to help locate some mark or position relative to other marks or positions. A surveyor constructs a diagram of the whole. He must use only a few dominant marks, directions, and connections to convey that wholeness or else produce a map of no use whatever. To teach a survey we must confront and use its inevitable artifice.

In a survey, the particulars are included as relational, representative landmarks. Our teaching must be relational: a text in its relations to other texts and to a wholeness of some kind—the wholeness being, like all mental constructs, an artifice. Our teaching must be dialectical: texts confront and oppose each other in a single space. Our teaching must be synecdochic: parts represent wholes and must be taught as samples. A sampler course may pretend to be merely a miscellany chosen from a certain segment of time, but a sampler samples something. We are uneasy with such artifices, but we must choose and teach our mental construct or not bother.

Choosing can be more rational if we reflect on our beliefs about literary history. Literature has a history: it should sometimes be studied in terms of how and why it changes. Literature is made in social and cultural contexts: sometimes it should be studied in relation to other activities representative of a place-time. Literature is a special way of viewing the world: sometimes it should be studied as an expression of a world view, or as a means of propagating or changing such a view. These three beliefs will operate as our criteria, taking precedence over other claims. Texts are chosen according to how well they serve the study of literary change and fashion, the study of literary-cultural coherence, the study of literature as world view. Other texts—too traditional or autonomous or eccentric—will, however valuable, be saved for other kinds of courses. Each of these criteria is an artifice with its own dangers, but artifice is inescapable. Let's look at them one at a time.

In "Innovation and Variation," Ralph Cohen helps define our first problem. First, "history must be segmented in order to be comprehensible" (3). The slices we make in time are arbitrary in some degree, but we must make them for heuristic purposes. Second, the study of history means the study of change, and we must understand kinds of change. When we study a past period, we generally begin with the familiar question, "What's new?" This is paradoxical, for most students come to a past expecting "what's old." Our primary aim is to help them discover the newness of a past. To reveal the newness of a past, we overemphasize (as we must) innovation, the sense that something new is happening, that one is living in a time of change. Inevitably we pick or make segments of time when change and innovation seem most pronounced—moments that seem revolutionary.

If revolutionary moments are what we teach, then we must explore what revolution is and how it works. Revolution generates reaction, and so reaction must also be studied—not as a merely negative concept (the way Romantics were once taught as revolutionaries who went wrong). We also teach that innovation includes continuity, and revival of something lost or slighted. Newness includes a new sense of the past—as "renascence" implies—and revival implies improvement, as in restoring a house. To revive the past is to rewrite it: Renaissance rewrites Graeco-Roman; neoclassicism rewrites classic; Romanticism rewrites romance, the medieval. Change is textual revision of the past world. We must teach these rather difficult ideas as instruments for studying literary change. Such is our rule model of pedagogy.

A second problem, teaching the cultural coherence of literature, presents its own artifices. Obviously we cannot include all cultural manifestations and must choose. Suppose we select the cultural activities called arts. Alastair Fowler gives us a balanced assessment of the advantages: "Only when we have referred a literary work to its social and artistic matrix of patronage, fashion and period tendency can we fully grasp its individual qualities [if then]. Now, in this attempt comparisons between the arts give valuable help, by sharpening our sense of period" (488). Students would, I think, testify to the excitement they felt upon discovering that different arts express the same cultural situation. Fowler finds unusual heuristic value in the concept of a period style. Our problem is the difficulty of teaching style at all to many of our students. How can we teach analogies among Augustan versification, Palladian architecture, rococo music and decor until students understand the styles of Augustan verse? Structural linguists may teach that the arts of a period reflect shared syntactic models. But first our students will need a better understanding of syntax.

I take an easier way and focus instead on *mode*. By mode I mean a distinctive general way of selecting, representing, and responding to perceived reality: comic, tragic, naturalistic, and so on. Read "mode" for "form" in the following:

> *How* a given form of literary work appeared as it did, *where* it did, and *when* it did, these are the problems that historians must solve. Solutions to these problems will determine the range of possible answers given to the more important questions of *why* a given form of literature appeared where, when, and how it did. (White 99)

A focus on mode has several pedagogical advantages. For one, it correlates with modes of the student's own responses. For another, modes are continuities: each moment in cultural history has its own *versions* of pastoral and fantasy, tragedy and comedy. For a third, mode cuts across generic and formal lines: poems, plays, and novels may be tragic; lyric, drama, and narrative may be pastoral. Finally, modes transcend differences of media: comic, pathetic, pastoral apply to music, painting, sculpture as well as to literature. Certain versions of certain modes prevail at certain times in taste and fashion. The causes may be explicable.

The causes are not just aesthetic. Students, Scholes writes, "must see naturalism and aestheticism not simply as styles or modes of production in an isolated realm of art, but as world views with social consequences" (38). Variant modes are expressive of a world view peculiar to a period. The world-view approach to a literary period has its own advantages and risks. It emphasizes ways of perceiving and ordering the world, world images, world metaphors. It emphasizes cosmos, the wholeness implicit in a particular, the world in a grain of sand. One danger is that we make the world view too philosophical to apply to a human majority. Another is that we make it too coherent to allow for individual differences. We may also make it too distinct, cloaking overlaps and similarities. We should not allow the impression that world view is identical with world as experienced; rather, it is a response (perhaps hostile or antithetical) to it. The rage for order in the Renaissance reflects an anxious sense of contemporary disorder. The prizing of rationality in the Enlightenment, the prizing of morality in the Victorian period, is the inverse side of perilous balance, of the dark underside of Victorian life. Finally, world views are most discernible in the process of change, when challenged or threatened. If change is part of our subject, we must show world views changing or being challenged. The so-called Augustan period is a time when Augustanism is competing with what is established and what will succeed it; the so-called Renaissance, Romantic, Modern periods are, too.

These are the terms that normally title our period surveys. The titles, however necessary, are misleading, of course. They are not historical, but ideological. The misleading implication is that a period in culture is the same as a dominant or new ideology. The Augustan period was not dominantly Augustan, nor the Romantic period dominantly romantic, the Modern period modernist. More often, the ideology we teach was a counter-ideology. Literature often reflects or promotes a counter-culture, radical, conservative, or both. Nonetheless, the use of such titles, if we take them seriously (and if not, why not change the titles?), commits us to teaching literature ideologically, and some teachers will want to do—or think they *can* do—otherwise. All literature is ideological, whatever else it may be; but in some periods the most influential or innovative writers *intend* literature to be ideological, and in others they don't. An exclusively ideological focus makes difficult the comparison with other arts. If Romantic music is not a music of idea, painting not a painting of ideas (even though people had ideas about them), I can hardly teach Romantic literature in its coherence with other arts if I emphasize only ideological content, "thematics." Instead, I will emphasize modes of imagining the world, knowing and showing that they have ideological consequences.

Many students believe that they are Romantics; few think of themselves as Augustans or Victorians. Courses with a focus on modes and ideologies that retain a strong appeal will be approached quite differently than courses in modes and ideologies that seem alien. My example in what follows must therefore be a special case. I will try, as before, to suggest a design and a pedagogy that are adaptable to period courses in general. But you should be aware of an ideological bias, and I should acknowledge it in teaching. Students flock to courses with Romantic titles; the idea has lasting appeal. I see Romanticism as a dangerous ideology, momentous, undeniably influential, but in some ways distasteful and deluded. My bias must be confessed: we must try to understand its power and importance, but we must also realize its dangers. We will criticize it. We will immerse ourselves in it. Can we do both?

Certainly not at the same time, and not with an overbalance on the critical side. In *Textual Power*, Scholes argues that what we most owe our students in this "age of manipulation" is the critical power to resist, to adopt an opposing ideological stance from which to criticize the cultural codes or values of texts. The "textual power" he writes of is chiefly a dangerous power to be resisted, and the "whole function of criticism" is to provide a way *out* of it. I disagree. My first obligation—and it is not easily met—is to provide a way *into* the power of Romanticism. The pedagogy described below reflects this emphasis. But the course design embodies a critical distance, ways out. Design and pedagogy must play dialectically against each other, moving us in and out in alternation.

II

First, here is the design in brief. Expect to be startled or dismayed by what is left out and even by what is put in. The explanations will follow.

I.	(One week)	Reading a Romantic Text. Coleridge's "Kubla Khan," Keats's "Urn," Shelley's "Mont Blanc."
II.	(Three sessions)	Ideas of Art and Society. Brief selections in a photocopied text,

		grouped by Art and Society, paired according to common issues.
III.	(One session; 75 minutes)	Samples of Romantic Art and Music.
IV.	(3-1/2 weeks)	The *Gothic* Mode. Godwin, *Caleb Williams;* Blake, selections from *Innocence and Experience, Marriage of Heaven and Hell,* one short "historical" prophecy.
V.	(3-1/2 weeks)	The *Romantic* Mode. Scott, *Ivanhoe;* Byron, selections from *Childe Harold* III and IV; *Manfred;* selections from *Don Juan.*
VI.	(3-1/2 weeks)	The *Pastoral* Mode. Austen, *Persuasion;* Wordsworth, selections from *The Prelude;* half a dozen lyrics and sonnets; *Ode: Intimations of Immortality.*

The "content" is controversial. Most controversial must be the decision to give so much time to novels in a period traditionally taught (like many period courses) for its poetry and poetics. The issue is special to the period, but similar unpleasant choices must be made in every survey course. Such courses often emphasize poetry, abandoning narrative and drama to their own generic surveys, giving false impressions of the periodicity of all three. Novelists and dramatists are at least as much "in period" as poets; poets in every period work in generic traditions. We must try to show that they all reflect the same cultural situation. By pairing a poet with a novelist three times, I am choosing to stress this objective. To do so, I must slight some major poets. I compensate by using them in opening sessions, and in excerpts about art and society. Students are invited, from the start, to study them in individual or group projects.

I have several reasons for beginning with three poems. First, we must start off with a focus on the problems and processes of reading. Second (and this is crucial), we begin to see that reading changes from period to period, that the reader's roles change historically, that we as readers are part of this history. Third, out of this first study, we can make some tentative hypotheses about what to expect, the whatness and whyness of literature in this period that warrant giving it a collective name. Consider the three "subjects": a fantastic palace, a timeless artwork, and a sublime natural form. Consider the situations in which these "others" are confronted and addressed. Do they have common qualities or appeals? Do the interactions have anything in common? Each experience moves through certain tensions or conflicts to some climax or resolution. Can we find any common terms to describe the movements? Each generates "lessons" or messages. Do the poems intend to teach? Are the messages similar? Let's add up our answers and consider whether there is a justification for placing the three poems under a single epochal rubric.

Following this first exercise in reading, we come to the preparatory sessions (Item II in the plan) on Art and Society, using brief photocopied excerpts, the first group dealing with art and poetry, the second (from Lamb, Hazlitt, Cobbett, Wollstonecraft et al.) dealing with ideas and images of society. Romantic poetic theory is, of course, complex and prolix, and we will be in search of only a few key ideas and issues. Social debate less so. But these are only preliminary sessions, prior to our major triad of paired authors. So the initial pedagogy is didactic; the teacher does lots of focusing and expounding. As the course goes on, and the ideas are concretely tested and reinforced in our chief authors, they will assume more vital meanings. The questions below, for these "excerpt" sessions, are general enough to apply to other periods as well.

1. The question of what is art focuses on what special powers make an artist. What key terms repeat? Closely related is the question of how art is created. Do we find any shared views of the processes of creation?

2. What is art about? Do we find any similar answers, any basic disagreements? Do their answers differ from ours?

3. What is art for? What kind of value is it supposed to

have, and for whom? Do the excerpts offer any similar answers, and do our own answers differ?

4. What kinds of art do these writers seem to hold most valuable? Can we figure out why? Do our own preferences differ, and if so, why?

  (End of discussion, with a closing warning: theory and practice often do not coincide or even agree. Don't expect all we read to "carry out" the ideas we have been identifying.)

The excerpts of prose about society and social ideas that then follow must serve more than one purpose. In so selective a course, every text has to play several roles. The chief aim of this group of excerpts is to suggest meaningful connections between ideas of art and ideas of society. After all, the interplay of art and society is one of the chief subjects of any such course. My agenda must be special, but a similar agenda could be designed for any period.

1. Contemporaries saw themselves living through historical change and felt a peculiar sense of the past. Compare Sydney Smith's view of progress and improvement with Charles Lamb's view of the past in the present. Are you reminded of any of our ideas about art?

2. Many were aware of living through revolutions. But revolution from what, against what, to what? Compare Wollstonecraft's revolutionary values with those of Cobbett. Any common ideals and common enemies? Are you reminded of any revolutionary ideas about art we have just studied?

3. People had a new consciousness of social bonds, pressures, obligations. What are some fundamental differences between Burke's view of society and Godwin's? How might Smith, Lamb, Wollstonecraft, and Cobbett align themselves in this disagreement? How about our art writers?

4. Many felt a strong new commitment to the values we call individualism. Compare Lamb's ideal of the free, self-

contained man with Hazlitt's ideal of powerful individual temperament. Are our other writers equally individualistic? What do our art theorists say about the values of individuality?

(End of session. The pedagogy depends heavily on the heuristic of dialogue. Discrete texts are made to talk to each other, and our emphasis is on their disagreements. This artifice will carry us through the weeks to come.)

In a final preparatory session, examples of painting and music are shown and heard. No attempt is made to give a technical account. The aim is merely to evoke impressions of qualities shared by literary texts: in content, iconography, scale; in texture, mood, rhythm. The groupings anticipate the three-mode construct of major authors: (1) the period's gothic taste for the weird, the terrible, the irrational; (2) the period's romantic taste for the exotic, the adventurous, the primitive; (3) the period's pastoral taste for the natural, tranquil, stable. These are not mere aesthetic tastes; they are related to world views with social consequences.

Nor are they to be presented as discrete stages or schools. How easy it was to learn (?) the Renaissance as an orderly sequence from Spenserian to Metaphysical to Jonsonian! How difficult to understand that Pope, Defoe, and Sentimental Steele all reflected the same cultural situation! We want to learn a unity of period, but we also must learn that any period is a coexistence of overlapping and conflictive modes and codes. Some initial confusion is inevitable and probably useful. These warnings follow us into our triad of pairs: Godwin and Blake; Scott and Byron; Austen and Wordsworth.

The first pair represents the most radical and least fashionable strain. The second represents the most fashionable of tastes. To study literature as an institution, we must study fashion and taste, how they change in history; we must study audience, and so we must not exclude "best-sellers." The third pair represents what seems so far the most enduring: Austen and Wordsworth had late impacts, and their classic status is the least questioned. Every period might be modeled on such a scheme. It obviously requires a nonchronological order; I play fast and loose with chronology in order to emphasize period unity, which is my chosen artifice.

In pedagogy, I try to redress the imbalance. I teach texts as representative samples, but do not distort them to such a degree that they can have no other mode of existence. No writer ever sat down to write a representative text. I teach texts as responses to a shared social-historical situation, but this is too "one-way." Text and situation interact: text creates situation, as situation creates text. I teach texts as imaginative interactions, and some students confuse them with documentaries. One advantage of Romantic texts, of course, is that they are difficult to confuse with documentary realism; they work by idealizing or transforming. Indeed, my pedagogical problem is the opposite: how to reveal that such texts are interactive at all with sociohistorical reality.

The remedy is in the dialectical design. Different texts respond differently, and as we compare them, the situation they respond to emerges. Here, for example, is the blueprint of one discussion: All see the world of experience into which one inevitably falls from innocence. How do images of "the world" differ and what do they share? What is innocence in its variants, and why must it fall? Do innocence and its fall vary from mode to mode?

We slide here into a popular emphasis in teaching Romantic literature: myth, symbolic story pattern. The emphasis may be tempting in other periods as well. The prevalence of seemingly narrative texts on my list invites such an emphasis; the dominance of story patterns in students' expectations encourages it. Structuralist theory endorses it. It is more or less adaptable to any period. But I want to play it down. It puts too great a premium on plot and character. As narrative it distorts the ambiguity of time in Romantic texts. It blurs dramatic and lyric patterns, blocks comparisons with other arts, slights non-narrative structures such as state, mood, situation.

I will stress situation instead. We are studying a moment in flux, and we will try to grasp its unity as a situation. An emphasis on situation works better pedagogically if our primary aim is access to the period, getting "into" it. We see texts as interactions with a situation, and they offer versions of the situation powerful enough to draw us in, to make us (as Ortega would say) temporary provincials or villagers. So each text provides its own access to the situation that generated Romanticism, and we will ask— whether of narrative, lyric, or dramatic—such questions as these: What is the situation of Blake's voice or state of experience in "London"? Of Byron's Harold in the Alps? Of Caleb in flight? Of Ivanhoe in disguise? Of Anne at Bath? Of Wordsworth at his "naked pool" in *Prelude* XII? What have the situations in common? How do they diverge from or oppose each other? My teaching emphasis here is impersonative, identifying as much as possible with situations and states.

What we find is that the situations are characterized by conflict and division—with the world, within the self. Every period, Georg Lukacs tells us, is characterized by its own internal tensions and conflicts, and literature embodies them in consciousness. Conflict and division of consciousness make the situation more painful, more dramatic, and hence more powerfully appealing and accessible for the student reader. They draw us in. But they also provide a way out.

I agree with Scholes that outness is part of the game, and that we can achieve the outness, the vantage point from which to uncover and assess an ideology or world view, only by adopting an opposing ideology. Thus, when students (as often is the case) come to the course believing themselves Romantics, I have the task of prodding them into a more critical awareness even as I seek first to immerse them. They too are divided. They discover some of the more fearful or objectionable implications of "being romantic," discover they are something else. The repeated encounter with division and conflict provokes this. The design helps. The pairs operate dialectically. What they share matters, of course, but their antipathies or differences matter too. Godwin and Blake are both gothic revolutionaries, with shared values but with profound differences. Byron and Scott espouse and exploit romantic values and tastes, but as rivals with very different standpoints. Wordsworth and Austen celebrate pastoral values, but how different are their versions of nature, stability, and tranquillity! We are aided by one historical fact about romantic writers—perhaps about authors in any shared cultural situation: they are profoundly at odds with each other. In personality and temperament, to be sure, but more than that. Each saw the other as somehow untrue or antagonistic to the new vision. Each would revise the others. Byron is the most powerfully Romantic phenomenon of the time, but then why did Blake find him a fallen prophet in the wilderness, and Wordsworth find him a despot of the eye, and Austen treat him as a destabilizing, delusive influence? And why would he in turn treat the Wordsworth "school" as vaporous madmen and bores?

These heated conflicts within a single cultural phenomenon help us teach the diversity within any such unity. We can find comparable responses to a shared cultural situation, but each author has his or her "idiolect," particular idiom and vision. Each of them felt at times an "outsider" to the dominant new code or vision, and so we must be occasional outsiders as well.

Moreover, these writers are often at conflict with themselves, and the conflicts are often manifest in the texts they write. Many of our texts are unusually fragmentary, incoherent, unstable, and hardly warrant the sort of reverence that Scholes sees as a "legacy of romantic aestheticism." We needn't be radical deconstructionists to discover their blindspots, shifts, and incoherences, and to find in these some essential clues and keys to meaning. We can understand such imperfections and still revere the efforts of the worker-writer to respond to, interact with—even redeem—the world as perceived. Reading them this way, we can ask such questions as these:

Blake wrote *Songs of Experience* after *Songs of Innocence* and kept trying to rearrange them so as to suit his idea of the two titles. He placed "London" and "Tyger" as both expressive of a state called Experience. Do they really belong together in this way? Godwin was a secular rationalist who believed that reason was the best guide in social obligations.

But the finale of his novel is often read as a religious myth in terms that Godwin could not have accepted. Can we understand the finale as consistent with what has gone before?

Scott appeals to a taste for what is strange or different in the past, and yet he suggests that people are basically the same in all periods. Does either of these beliefs prevail? In *Childe Harold* III, Byron's hero seeks and fails to find a oneness with nature. In *Childe Harold* IV, the hero has disappeared, and Byron is seeking oneness with eternal monuments of art and mind. Can these be from the same author? Wordsworth could never stop rewriting *The Prelude,* and so we have a text that is really several layers combined. He includes several versions of his "fall." Where do they differ? Does the poet ever successfully return to nature? Austen's *Persuasion* was left unrevised when she died. What scenes should have been included or developed that aren't, and what scenes could have been omitted or summarized that aren't?

III

A reverential attitude toward the text may or may not be a Romantic legacy. The deconstructive attitude is certainly a romantic legacy, and it must be part of our teaching in any period survey. Writers working in a cultural situation cannot create texts without conflict and contradictions. But the chief end of a period survey, however artificial, is the discovery that there is such a thing as a distinctive and explicable period literature, related to other cultural activities, reflective of the shared cultural situation. So our pedagogical ending must be affirmative and synthetic.

My original ending for this chapter described the finale of the course. The teacher synthesized (and reviewed) all the course's themes and variations through an anatomy of Wordsworth's Immortality Ode. This closure comforted some students, excited others, and embarrassed the teacher. Here, I end instead with a confession. Such a performance is not hard to do, and it may well be defensible as a summarizing strategy. But the Ode as poem was scarcely alluded to. Most students didn't object; many of these Romantics found poetry alien or frightening anyway. They liked the teacher for assigning some novels. They never knew it, but in a real sense they had failed the course, and perhaps the teacher had, too. When it comes to the special nature of poetry, our problem of art and artifact, of aesthetic object and social-historical context, remains unsolved.

SEVEN

The Strangeness of Poetry

I

    I have finessed the toughest challenge for teaching the survey—for me, anyway. Such courses include, even emphasize, lyric poetry. The challenge is dual. First, the poem is—at least it has seemed—the least contextual, the most autonomous, of texts. New Critical ideas of the autonomous text were modeled on the poem; play and novel were read as poems. Second, the poem has seemed the most alien and forbidding of forms to many of our students.

    Teaching Freshman Composition many years ago, I was confronted one day by a living poem. One of the three obligatory quarters in our year "used" literary texts. As our first session of using poems ended, a male student approached hesitantly. He was a member of the wrestling team, looked it every inch, and talked hesitantly. He glanced over one enormous shoulder, waited till we were alone, and asked if he could speak to me for a moment. I expected some horrid confession, and I got it. "I had to tell you," he muttered, "that I really *love* poetry! Sometimes back at the dorm I even lie on my bed and read it!" The sensual intimacy and the terror of exposure said it all.

    Twenty-eight years later I offered an advanced course in Scottish literature. Naturally, poetry was part of it, and I anticipated that this would scare off *some* majors and panic some of those who stayed. So, I made a survey, and the statements collected could probably be replicated in many other literature courses. "The difficulty is in finding the theme or point"; "Poetry in itself, being in that it is compact and concentrated, sometimes is so well packed that the point or theme cannot be dug out"; "My phobia of poetry stems from my deficiency to [*sic*] uncover the hidden meanings which the poet is trying to express, *if any*" [emphasis added]; "I can't always understand what exactly the poet is saying"; "It is not *immediately apparent* [emphasis added] what the author is trying to say"; "Many times when I've done what it takes to understand a poem [note words and order of events], the *last* thing I'm able to do is go back and read it with any *feeling*"; "Being unintimidated enough to relax and allow it to speak to me"; "The insecurity that if I don't infer the meaning of life from every poem then there's something wrong with me"; "I have a hard time understanding 'meanings' or 'symbolisms' in poems"; "Taught in high school like a dead frog in biology class."

I remember well (after thirty-five years) a group tutorial of sophomores trying to cope with Milton's sonnet on his late espoused Saint, led by a neophyte Teaching Fellow—me. The script has faded up to a point, a dramatic point, at which one young woman broke in and with exasperation declared, "Well, this is all *just words* to me!" The revelation that hit me has neither faded nor changed. "That's it!" I heard myself shout. "Poetry is just words!" What I have relearned repeatedly ever since is how many majors in literature are unnerved by "just words" and by the passionate and playful attention to words that makes poetry and the reading of poetry strange.

A passionate attention to "just words" is surely basic to any teaching of poetry. Once in a hallway I was advising a pre-law student, when a colleague in political science happened by. A lawyer himself, he taught courses in law and justice. I grabbed him and asked, "Jack, what kind of course should I recommend?" Without hesitation, he answered, "A course in poetry." "Why?" "Because nowhere else can you learn such a close attention to words." I suspect such advice is often followed. Once, when I observed a friend teaching Introduction to Poetry, many of his students sounded like lawyers. A student was asked to pick one of the assigned poems and read it aloud. The reading was often bad, or inappropriate, but no comment was made. Instead, the teacher gave his own reading, in a fine, emphatic, theatrical voice. And then, immediately, the questions were put: What is it about? What does it mean? The pre-lawyers took over, and with lively intensity debated the interpretation of words. No attempt was made to correlate the way the poem was read aloud with that other kind of interpretation, the sound with the sense.

Some teachers of poetry will see nothing abnormal here. They were trained in the same way. In *The Perception of Poetry* (1983), Eugene Kintgen studies a group of graduate students engaged in the act of reading poems. The act, he concedes, is atypical—but is it really? It is a "professional and pre-aesthetic preparation for talking about a poem." Highly revealing is the equation of professional and pre-aesthetic, the assumption that understanding precedes aesthetic response. The act is "doing things to poems," applying "interpretive strategies" toward "literary cognition." The object is to arrive at "a complete understanding of this poem." The model is problem-solving. Once the poem is "completely understood," then we are ready for the aesthetic, ready for pleasure. It may be unnecessary to explain how this act, this sequence, is inimical to what most theorists have considered the very nature of poetry. (I will recall their views later.) The point here is that many dedicated teachers of poetry were once these graduate students.

I tested Kintgen's findings in a graduate seminar in the teaching of literature. The course opened with a comparative hearing of two ballads. I then asked the group: (1) What words would you use to distinguish between the main feelings you got from the two stories? (2) Which story had more value for you, and what kind of value did it have more of? The discussion proceeded nervously, until some anxious souls asked me, "When will we get down to the question of meaning?", and a few confessed that reading and talking about poetry my way made them quite jumpy.

Our discussion necessarily turned to the question with which any teacher of poetry nowadays must begin: Why is there such widespread resistance to poetry, even among students of literature? Why is it, as Donald Stauffer asked years ago, that "the average adolescent or adult (for children know what poetry is) feels uncomfortable or irritated or bored when he confronts a poem" (12–13)? Stauffer's answers are still heard: the easy substitutes of the media; rapid reading; the prevalence in our culture of the eye. Others might be added: cultural attitudes toward language (the strict separation of words and things), cultural distrust of emotive language, the teaching of reading as a linear process, and the teaching of literature as dominantly narrative. Our students bring narrative norms to all reading; the words of a poem must convey an episode or express a character. One must then figure out (or imagine) a narrative context; if one can do this, the poem is transformed into something else; if one can't, frustration follows—it is all "just words." What is the teacher of poetry to do? How will we begin?

II

I'll begin here with a choice of three poems: Frost's "Stopping By Woods," Blake's "London," and "Culloden and After" by the Scottish poet I. C. Smith. (The text of this unfamiliar poem is given later in the chapter.) I teach them in this order, not simply because it is the order of relative difficulty, but also because this sequence best fits our Whitehead rhythm. With "Stopping," we begin in a predisciplinary mode; with "London," we stress precision; with "Culloden," we face the problems of context.

For beginning a class, Kasulis recommends a warm-up of "fact" questions. Nancy Hoffman recommends a warm-up of group problem-analysis. Here I'll reject both. The "fact" beginning—how many stanzas? what metrics or rhyme schemes?—signals that these are of primary importance. The "problem" beginning signals that the poem is to be "solved." I'll begin instead from John Hollander's notion that every poem is "in the ear" and "in the eye," a counterpoint of seeing and hearing. I'll begin from my belief that the real *elements* of language in a poem are three: texture (seen and felt), rhythm (heard and felt), and voice (heard and overheard, heard as if spoken by me as I read). "Just words" are heard in patterns, and we have to feel the patterns first.

Here are some possible first questions to ask about Frost's "Stopping." Which might serve best for a starter, and why? (1) Do you like this poem? Why? Why not? (2) When and where does the poem take place? (3) What kind of person is the speaker? (4) What happens? (5) What's the rhyme scheme and what's the metre? (6) What does the horse stand for? (7) What promises does the speaker have to keep? (8) Have you ever found yourself in a situation *like* this? How did *you* feel?

Number 1 could work if we knew how to follow up on the answers we would probably receive: It sounds good; it's simple; it's about nature; it's inspiring; I can identify with this person; it reminds me of a time when I. . . . But the follow-ups would probably become abstract and argumentative. Numbers 2, 3, and 4 misrepresent the nature of a poem: it's not a narrative or dramatic event. Number 5 is premature; first, we would have to identify our sensations of rhythm and voice. Numbers 6 and 7 jump prematurely to interpretive generalizations. Number 8 would serve me best, for "situation" comes closest to the poem's given, and our quickest access is by way of association. But the situation is revealed only in and through the speaker's feelings about it, and the feelings are conveyed only through rhythms and voices. So, we would start with efforts to identify this surface of rhythm and voice. If we can realize the patterns of sound (a good Frost dictum), the sense will follow. Here are the questions I ask:

> In this poem of watching, what is actually seen? Why so late and so little? Why is the watching of snow interrupted by the thought of a horse thinking? What's the negative feeling of the echoing queer-near-lake-mistake-shake? Why stop here at all? The shaking is opposed rhythmically to the stopping. If we can feel the growing tension between stopping and going, we will realize what is "happening." The horse's challenge is displaced by different sounds, an opposing voice, a sound felt in sweep and easy. Can you really *hear* a downy

flake? Can you really *see* lovely, dark, and deep? In your *mind*? The effect is of a strange, hypnotic watching-hearing that reaches a rhythmic climax in "lovely, dark, and deep," then is sharply broken by the force of BUT I, and the "I" repeatedly asserts itself. Changing and competing rhythms can be heard here as changing and competing voices: the I who thinks and knows uneasily; the I who hears a warning in a horse's bell; the I who forgets itself in dark, deep, sweep, and flake; the I who recalls itself to . . . motion? to . . . ? Say the poem aloud again, trying to get the voice "right" at each stage, stanza, shift. Try out various voicings of the final stanza. Which voicings best convey the shifting states of feeling and consciousness that the poem takes us through?

Our attempts to decide inevitably lead to questions of "meaning": the woods, village, darkness, invisibility, uneasy conscience, promises. Few poems better illustrate Kenneth Burke's distinctions—"Drama is dissolved in turn from dramatic *act* to lyric *state*" (qtd. in Styan 1)—or Riffaterre's belief that in a poem we "hurdle the mimesis" (2)—the representational impulse of narrative—to come at the "significance."

With poems at this first, predisciplinary stage, we are postponing formal and technical scrutiny to discover how a poem "works" and how we readers get "into" these workings. With the next stage, and stranger and more difficult poems such as Blake's "London," I need to become more didactic and precise. The voice of "London" sounds very different from the "Stopping" voice because the rhythms are different, and yet metrically and stanzaically they are the "same." Scansion will reveal the sameness, and we must learn to scan. Why is this voice so much louder and more strident? We notice the prevalence of stress-opened lines, the hammering patterns of alliteration, the double-beats or spondees, the iteration, that make this a "marching" poem as distinct from Frost's stopping and pausing poem, faster, harsher. The end-stopped lines are sharper than Frost's softer, briefer end-stops, and they stress the strong rhyme words.

This hearing is radically different from "the sweep / Of easy wind and downy flake." This is visionary hearing; the metaphoric identities, like the grammar, defy prose logic. How can a sigh run down a wall? What is a blackening church? How can a curse blight, and what is a marriage hearse? In sum, to identify the very different effects of "London," we need a terminology to use, we need names for metrics and figures and forms. We are at the stage for this kind of precision. We are trying to identify and understand the special kinds of things poets do with words. We can then refer the poem back to its own social and political world.

In a third and final stage, we broaden the perspective to confront problems of context—historical, cultural, ideological, biographical—and the poems are chosen accordingly. Smith's "Culloden and After" is suitably challenging in this respect.

> You understand it? How they returned from Culloden
> over the soggy moors aslant, each cap
> at the low ebb no new full tide could pardon:
> how they stood silent at the end of the rope
> unwound from battle: and to the envelope
> of a bedded room came home, polite and sudden.
>
> And how, much later, bards from Tiree and Mull
> would write of exile in the hard town
> where mills belched English, anger of new school:
> how they remembered where the sad and brown
> landscapes were dear and distant as the crown
> that fuddled Charles might study in his ale.
>
> There was a sleep. Long fences leaned across
> the vacant croft. The silly cows were heard
> mooing their sorrow and their Gaelic loss.
> The pleasing thrush would branch upon a sword.
> A mind withdrew against its dreamed hoard
> As whelks withdraw or crabs their delicate claws.
>
> And nothing to be heard but songs indeed
> while wandering Charles would on his olives feed
> and from his Minch of sherries mumble laws.

The poem obviously assumes historical familiarity, and my students will not have it. There is nothing wrong with imparting the needed information; informing is a legitimate part of teaching. The question is when and how. If I give in to student perplexity and do so first, I place a counter-text—the story of the battle, of Charles, of the Clearances—between reader and reading. If I offer fragmentary glosses, footnotes, I lose the poem's impact in topicality. If I translate the poem into "history," I insulate the student comfortably from the poem's essential strangeness. So, I try to guide us through our earlier stages—the questioning we did with Frost, the close rhythmic and imagistic scrutiny we did with Blake. "Understanding it" is postponed, as in fact the poem postpones understanding. Then I offer the counter-text, Culloden as an experience, and ask what the poem is really about.

This is not the place for explication, but a few general hints are appropriate to our present purpose. The poem opens, "You understand it?" and no definition of "it" can be realized without thinking and feeling our way through the poem. It is a poem of memory; prosodically and metaphorically, all is framed in a sad and vacant completion. This is not Culloden; this is "after," and "after" is a matter of attitude, not fact. What emerge as most strange are the attitudes, the responses, to this terrible loss or dispossession. Most striking is the absence of anyone—anyone but the "you"—to feel these responses. Out of the strangeness there forms an attitude; the "it" is an attitude. Do "you" understand it at last? The poem suggests that no full understanding is possible. Poems often end with such a suggestion.

The essential thing is the absence of "I." Instead, a "you" is voiced, a "you" thinks. It is I the reader. This is the strange intimacy of poetry. Our wrestler sensed it. Georges Poulet (in another connection) described it:

> You are inside it; it is inside you; there is no longer either outside or inside . . . I am aware of a rational being, of a consciousness; the consciousness of another, no different from the one I automatically assume in every human being I encounter, except that in this case the consciousness is open to

me, welcomes me, lets me look deep inside itself, and even
allows me, with unheard of license, to think what it thinks
and feel what it feels . . . The work lives its own life within
me; in a certain sense, it thinks itself, and it even gives itself
a meaning within me. (53)

Indeed, the same is true in our other two poems; the I there
is also a "you," a consciousness open for appropriation, an intimate "other" that the reader becomes. This is the strangeness
of poetry.

Shall we teach so as to explain away the strangeness? Or shall
we heed the advice of Howard Nemerov?

Much of education proceeds, and rightly, by making the
strange familiar, interpreting the unknown in terms of the
known, and so on, which is more or less what we mean by
explaining something . . . But I wish now to consider the opposite process, and suggest that a part of teaching ought to
consist in making the familiar strange. That at least would be
the normal way of saying it, but as so often happens the normal way of saying it is wrong, being not strange enough itself.
Rather than "making the familiar strange," which suggests
strangeness appliqued onto familiar substance, I shall say
"revealing the strangeness that is already there." (106)

III

What and why is this strangeness? Bear with me
while I summarize what I hope students of poetry will finally
learn. If this summary slights the usual "elements," it does so because the elements are not elemental enough. My elements are
these: texture, rhythm, and voice. The whatness I aim at is
nothing new. It is the same whatness emphasized in recent theoretical writing about poetry. This writing employs formidable
meta-languages, but I find such suggestive power in some of their
phrases that I will quote them. If the language seems strange, the
strangeness is necessary.

(1) The language of a poem is strange, and "making strange"

is its aim. As readers we receive signals that "this is something to be read carefully," because poets, says Wallace Stevens, "like words to sound wrong" (Cardinal 85, 88). They sound wrong because they are being used for their own sake, set apart from "everyday life and language" (Easthope 16). Put technically, "the function of poetic language consists in the maximum foregrounding of the utterance" (Mukarovsky, in Easthope, 16).

Poets view words as powers, naming or other-naming (metonym), magic (Skelton 18, 105, 113). Words are cut loose from their habitual references, and this introduces a "wandering or fuzziness into language" (Kristeva 133, 136). Most people have been taught to distrust wandering and fuzziness, and they consider "any evidence of instability as being an intrusion of some anarchic spirit into the language system" (Skelton 10). The loosing and foregrounding of words give words the peculiar semblance of things, "all but physical" (Easthope 15–16; Cardinal 98).

Word-things make a surface; they are there to be seen, not seen through. The surface is the way to enter. "Tennyson's surface," said Eliot (295), "his technical accomplishment, is intimate with his depths . . . By looking innocently at the surface we are most likely to come to the depths." Children are quite capable of such innocent looking. Adults are often deprived by critics and teachers who make "the lugubrious mistake—knowingly and deliberately—of neglecting the mushroom above the surface for detective excavations in the mycelium underneath . . . Yet nothing matters except the tint, the shape, the texture and the taste, the totality of each individual poem above the ground" (Grigson 186). The surface is texture, rhythm, and voice.

(2) Texture is touch-pattern. All the items in a poem are textured, woven together into patterns. A poem is "pattern-saturated" (Skelton 21), a network where every sign exists in relation to every other and to the nucleus or whole. A texture is a patterning in and of space. A poem on its surface is a textured space, and its words take on spatial quality. We read a poem not in the customary linear movement, but rather back and forth, in and around, following various interweaves. We feel the texture in various links and contrasts of look and feel—light and dark, thin

and thick, rough and smooth, tight and loose. The discovery of texture is the discovery of patterns or weaves. "Poems are words drawn and held together as if magnetically"; the "fitted words of poetry are magical or intoxicating" (Grigson 150, 78).

(3) The interweave discloses another strangeness. Every word fits into the texture, affects it, is affected in turn. Words woven together share meanings and associations. They borrow from each other, come into strange correspondences with each other. To read texturally is to come upon meanings borrowed, shared, displaced. This is the process we call metaphor. What matters is not some taxonomy of metaphors. What matters is realizing what the process is, how it happens, why poetry seems radically metaphoric: *meta*—over, change; *phor*—carry; *metaphor*—change by carry-over. The effect is strange, but the strangeness is no mere trick of indirection. It reveals a way of seeing reality, seeing the world as all-together in correspondences, a way that "regards all phenomena as being so closely related that they may be identified with each other, or seen and known through each other" (Skelton 39; Cardinal, Chapter 10).

(4) If texture is the patterning of space, rhythm is the patterning of time. Rhythm sets the language apart, foregrounds it. Rhythm is "one of the conditions of a poem existing all" (Whalley 204). It is "the fundamental force, the fundamental energy of verse . . . I know nothing of metre" (Myakovsky, qtd. in Grigson 11). Our students can "know nothing of metre" until they realize what rhythm is and how it works. Rhythm is everywhere in life, is life. It may begin in repeated sounds, but other kinds of repetition and variation follow. Rhythm makes a poem move even as it stands still; every poem is a counterpoint of stasis and movement. The time-pattern of a poem can be felt in its movements of echo and variation.

(5) Texture and rhythm are felt; otherwise, the poem's surface is not realized. Texture is seen, too, while rhythm is heard. Every poem is a counterpoint of seeing and hearing: the poem "in the ear" and the poem "in the eye" (Hollander). They interplay.

All that is heard is voice. Voice in and of a poem may sound singular, plural, multiple, or shifting. Let's not speak of a "speaker," for the notion may be misleading. It invites us to talk about "characters," to translate the poem into a drama or story, as if a poem were simply a story or a play *manqué*. It invites us prematurely to look for an individual "I" which can somehow be separated from the poem's utterance. Some poems say "I," some "we," some neither, some both. What speaks is the language (Easthope 31). And since the reader is the one who hears the language speaking, in a curious sense "only the reader speaks" (Easthope 24). The reader becomes the speaker: "The poem, because it is invariably of a *pseudo-dramatic* nature . . . forces us to indulge in a degree of impersonation; we are made to 'become' the poem" (Skelton 76, emphasis added).

But in what sense is (are) the poem's voice(s) heard? Many teachers and students agree that a poem must be "read aloud" to be realized, but this is a half-truth. In many poems, the speaking is silent, internal. Yes, "poems are always aloud, even if silently, always spoken, even if internally." But we speak "some of the words silently to ourselves, some of them aloud to ourselves," and so "the vocal performance needs to be on the personal stage, aloud and alone to yourself" (Grigson 195, 74, 147). Of what elements is voice made? Our students (and perhaps we ourselves) have little sense of voice, awareness of pitch, pace, duration, timbre, intonation, register, reverberation, overtone, and so on (Berry 9– 19). And yet, we and our textbooks expect to teach tone as a quality of voice without explaining voice, as the expression of an *attitude* without being too clear about what an attitude is.

(6) The culmination of a poem is an attitude; this is its "significance" or "meaning." We follow the all-togetherness of a voice (or voices) emerging through the surfaces of textures and rhythms, through the strange correspondences of words, and what we discover (in some degree acquire) is an attitude. An attitude is a way of perceiving that shapes and reshapes the perceiver and what is perceived. A poem closes as an act of perception that discovers or reveals a "vision of reality" (Whalley 235).

No one has said it better than Frost: "It begins in delight, it inclines to the impulse, it assumes direction with the first line laid down, it runs a course of lucky events, and ends in a clarification of life—not necessarily a great clarification, such as sects and cults are founded on, but in a momentary stay against confusion" (vi). It may involve "a glad recognition," but it must be "a revelation, or a series of revelations, as much for the poet as for the reader" (vii). This juxtaposition of recognition and revelation is crucial. If the poem simply allows a recognition, no revelation can follow. John Dewey makes this distinction between recognition and true perception, which is revelation. "Recognition is too easy to arouse vivid consciousness. There is not enough resistance between new and old to secure consciousness of the experience that is had" (Skelton 87). And Dewey: "Otherwise, there is not perception but recognition. The difference between the two is immense. Perception is an act of the going out of energy in order to receive" (Dewey 976–7). The Russian formalists define poetry in similar terms:

> [T]he essential function of poetic art is to counteract the process of habituation encouraged by routine everyday modes of perception. We very readily cease to "see" the world we live in, and become anesthetized to its distinctive features. The aim of poetry is to reverse that process, to *defamiliarize* that with which we are overly familiar, to "creatively deform" the usual, the norms, and so to inculcate a new child-like, nonjaded vision in us. The poet thus aims to disrupt "stock responses," and to generate a heightened awareness to restructure our ordinary perception of "reality," so that we end by *seeing* the world instead of numbly recognizing it. (Hawkes 62)

So here we are back with Nemerov where we began, back with the strangeness. If we can surrender to the strangeness, the poem will finally open onto the world and reveal it. But the revelation cannot come unless we begin with "the physical body of the poem," its surface, textures, rhythms, voices (Whalley 223). If our teaching does not begin there, we are missing the point.

EIGHT

The Idea of Performance

I

By its nature, a poem is performed in special ways; a play is, too, and the ways are basically different. Our performances as teachers must shift accordingly, and so must the performances of our students if they are to learn and we are to measure their learning.

Recalling Whitehead's rhythm, we begin here with a relatively simple play, Goldsmith's *She Stoops to Conquer,* which we can teach first at a predisciplinary stage. Turning to a non-simple play about simplicity, Wilder's *Our Town,* we will focus on the essential disciplines, the elements of the form. The most difficult example, Shakespeare's *Othello,* is saved for last, and with it we can consider the problems of context in teaching drama. A brief plan for teaching *She Stoops* will set the stage.

The aim of my questions should be clear enough, but let me summarize just in case. I am trying to arouse a preliminary, no doubt vague, awareness of what is special, what is definitively theatrical, about a play. We will name and define these qualities later. I want to draw attention to the essentially interactive or dialogic nature of character, to the definitive condition of illusion, to the concepts of role and gesture, to the special and privileged role of audience. Almost any play will serve, but *She Stoops* with its evident simplicity and plain artifice is especially suitable for beginnings. The qualities and conditions we begin to glimpse here will be dealt with more precisely and conceptually later on.

1. The situation is presented in a way basically different from a poem's way—consisting of a network of social relations and interactions. How would you describe the network, the roles, the interactions? What patterns do you notice? When interactions are faulty, what is the cause?

2. Illusions are important. We accept the illusion that the place onstage is really a house, an inn, a field. The people of the play also have illusions about where they are. Why does what appears a "home" to Hardcastle appear as an "inn" to his wife? How could the two visitors be sure it is an inn? Can we visualize how to set these scenes? What clues are we given? What clues show how Mrs. Hardcastle could believe the bottom of her garden to be a dangerous faraway common?

3. People are what they appear, and yet the appearance is often an illusion. We hear people described in contradictory ways, and then we see them ourselves. The Tony described by his mother is quite unlike the Tony described by his stepfather and the one described by Constance. When Tony describes his family to the strangers, they appear different. We see and hear about contradictory Hardcastles and Kates. Hastings and Tony describe contradictory Constances. Why do people appear so contradictory? Do we? Is life like this?

4. In theatre as in life, people play roles, and they expect others to play roles in certain ways. What differences of opinion do we find in the play as to what roles people should play and how? Social pressures, here as in life, force people to play dual or artificial roles. The play is filled with people playing roles, some of them skillfully and some of them badly. What does it take to perform a role well? Which are the best performers here, which the worst, and how so?

5. A role is performed in words, but also in clothing and gesture. People speak, dress, and gesture according to social situations. Others understand (or misunderstand) according to what assumptions they make about situations. Study the first dialogue between Marlowe and Hardcastle: the two misunderstand each other because they are making contradictory assumptions. Can you find other scenes in the play where the same thing happens? How do people use words in these scenes? What do they do to each other with words? Can you recall similar scenes from life?

6. Focus on Kate. Kate shows a willing ability to shift roles. In scenes with Marlowe, she modifies roles according to need. Compare her scenes with Marlowe. As director, how would you tell the actress to act: stand, move, gesture, speak? What motivates her to do this? Do her motives differ from Tony's? How would an audience feel about such role-shifting?

7. The role of audience in theatre is privileged. Scenes are played directly before us by different performers. They move in and out; we stay. They know the part, while we see the whole. We can put the parts together, see the pattern. Scenes are played after we are prepared for them; characters are described before we see them; strategies are revealed to us ahead of time. We are given scripts and then watch them performed. We know what to expect. What would be the effect on us if we did not receive such preparation? Characters are surprised, bewildered, but we are not. Why should we enjoy such superiority? Happenings are not funny to Marlowe, or Hardcastle, or Mrs. Hardcastle on the "common"; they suffer and we laugh. Why do we? Can you imagine how this comedy could be remade into tragedy?

Those are the questions. It is surprising how many plays they might suit. I cannot give the answers because I don't know what they will be. What the questions mean, and what answers we are ultimately aiming for, should become clear as we turn to a very different play.

II

        An Empty Stage in Half-light: Thornton Wilder's description of what we see as we enter the theatre and the theatricality of *Our Town*. It's not a bad description of the setting for teaching plays in a classroom.

In a recent seminar for would-be teachers, *Our Town* was one of our texts. It was George's turn to teach us, and George had taught the play often in high school and loved it. In our seminar, graduate students played the roles (badly) of introductory students. (How can a teacher teach without the capacity to play the role of student?) What happened often happens when a literature class tries to discuss a play as a text. The empty stage was quickly crowded with jostling concepts. Drama and theatre were shoved out of sight. George opened with a general question: if the play "says" there is something "universal," can we agree on what it is? Responses quickly generated two issues: (1) What is special about time in this play? (2) What is special about the role of the Stage Manager? George, an able stage manager, gently directed us toward examples of what he named "the manipulation of time" in the play.

A tension grew. Would we talk about time as a theme or time as a strategy? Message or medium? George wanted us to discover how the play's designs and strategies generate "theme." His "students" kept jumping into statements and counterstatements of "what the theme or meaning is." George's question was *how* the play has meaning. Behind that lurked the more fundamental question, "How does any play mean?"—which can sustain several readings, most important: "How does any *play* mean?" How do we move from an Empty Stage in Half-light to a sense of play as a medium? Our role-playing graduate students wanted to skip all that and talk about time as theme. They wanted to define the Stage Manager's role without first considering what it means (they were trying to do it themselves) to play a role. They wanted to debate interpretations without reference to performance or theatrical illusion. George's high school students might have engaged with the surface more innocently.

My own role in the seminar was to raise simpleminded questions: "What is a theme in literature anyway? Is it different in a play? How does one find it and teach students to find it? How many other themes are there in the play? [The list in response was endless.] How many themes can a play have before it blurs or disintegrates?" What is *most important* in *Our Town*? And that is the question the whole play asks. The play, claimed Wilder, was "an attempt to find a value above all price for the smallest events in our daily life" (xi). Can an attempt be a theme? Can it be stated as follows: "The smallest events in our daily life have a value above all price?" Or is it this: "Almost none of us ever *realizes* this value?" The term "theme" is being used haphazardly to refer to a concept representing human experience, a question about that concept, a search for the meaning of that concept, a statement about it.

Such a confusing struggle is no way to begin. Can I come up with a better plan? Let me set down a sequence of questions, and then explain my aims.

1. On an empty stage, a man watches us, speaks to us, creates a town before us—does not really show it to us but maps it for us to create. The only real things he uses are tables, chairs, trellises, and a ladder. What do they signify? Homes. Two homes. One of the doctor's family, the other of the newspaper editor's family. How can we learn what is important with so little? Why these families?

2. Before we hear speaking, we see people moving, stopping, gesturing. Are there any basic patterns in what they do? Do these tell us what's important? We watch them perform mimicries of actions: they pretend to have newspapers, milkbottles, dishes, chicken feed, beans. What's the effect on us of this performing? Does it signify anything important about their lives?

3. The first dialogue is between Doc Gibbs and the news-

boy. The next two involve the milkman with Doc Gibbs and with his wife; then come dialogues of two mothers with their children. How are these dialogues? What are people trying to do to each other through words? What do they mostly talk about? How do their actions perform what they talk about?

4. What time is it? How much time is "covered" by the first act? How much time does it take us to see it? What times are left out? Is time fast or slow? How do these people feel about time? Here are two statements you might make about act 1: (a) Time is the most important thing; (b) Time is unreal, an illusion. Which seems true? Can both be true?

5. Act 2 is made up chiefly of two ceremonies or rituals. How is the drugstore scene a ritual or ceremony? How about the wedding? How are they alike and how are they different? What makes a ritual or ceremony more "important" than a routine? You can't have a ritual, a ceremony, or a play without people to *play roles* in it. Why do these actors have such difficulty playing their roles?

6. We all have many roles to play in life. What does this mean? The actors in this play have roles to play, and some play them well, some not so well. Some feel uneasy about role-playing. Is *playing a role* a violation of who we "really are"? Do these people in the play feel a role conflict? The Stage Manager plays two roles in act 2, and several elsewhere. How would you describe them? Can one actor play several roles?

7. People keep asking, "What is important?" and disagreeing about answers. Do you see any change in meaning of "important" as the play goes on? What does the final act suggest about "all these terribly important things"?

8. The final scene in the play—the climactic scene—is Emily's return to the living in act 3. How does the entire play seem to lead up to it? Your job is to direct it—to plan how it should be performed on stage. Find your

cues in the script, and then tell the actors how to act and speak.

III

Bernard Beckerman finds "four impediments" to teaching the "distinctively dramaturgic features of Shakespeare's work." The same apply to teaching any dramatist. They include the problem of perceiving how dramatic language works, the relative unavailability of concrete illustrative performances, and the lack of a "satisfactory vocabulary with which to talk about the drama" (Edens 311–4). They are interdependent, and the first includes them all:

> First, we find it difficult to isolate the exclusively dramatic elements of a play. Traditionally, we are accustomed to discussing theme, by which term we sometimes mean topic, sometimes concept. We gravitate easily to the analysis of trope, imagery, and diction. We are ready to interpret a Shakespearian work by the light of psychoanalysis or theology. We can even read character without the restraints of context, abstracting the total being from the stage play so that the personality transcends its medium. But when we come to deal with what we consider to be the characteristic dramaturgic features of Shakespeare's plays, we do not exhibit so sure a touch. (309–10)

What do we want students to learn about distinctively dramaturgic features?

"Theatre" means *a place to see*, for shows and showing, as distinct from describing, narrating, explaining. Theatrical drama works by "visual idiom" (Styan 46), and in "the conception and in the communication of drama, the picture must always anticipate the words" (Styan 4). A play "seems to be happening before our eyes" (Esslin 110). Immediacy gives it the concreteness and enigma of real-life situations. The play as performed "is not a pretended *representation* of a state of affairs but the pretended state

of affairs itself" (Searle, qtd. in Elam 111). It is spectacle presented in a special place, traditionally a stage. What kind of place
is a stage? What makes a place a stage? Where do we find stages
in the real world? Is there a stage in the classroom? Why has it
proven so common over the centuries to see the world itself as
a theatre or a stage? What happens to us when we see life as
theatre or the classroom as stage?

If "theatre" derives from a place where spectacles are seen,
"drama" derives from "action." What people see in a theatre is
action, but what do we mean by action? What makes behavior
into an action? Drama means seeing actions performed in space,
movements in space, to and from, far and near; seeing in terms of
proxemics—what people signify by the ways they move in space.
It means reading gestures as communications. A dramatist writes
in a gestural language. "The language of the drama calls for the
intervention of the actor's body in the completion of its meanings" (Elam 142). What is a gesture, and how does a gesture express meaning? How can the configurations of bodies on stage
signify relationships?

A stage is a real place where we see real people perform real
actions, and yet the actions are mimed, mimicked, "acted"—they
are illusions, pretenses, lies. The young man playing Hamlet is
"playing"; this is a *play.* The chair he sits on is a real chair, but we
accept the illusion that it is a chair in a Danish castle centuries
ago. In the theatre, says Burns, "reality and illusion are shifting
terms. They do not denote opposites. Everything that happens
on the stage can be called real, because it can be seen and heard
to happen. It is perceived by the senses and is therefore as real as
anything that happens outside the theatre" (15). But it is real only
as an appearance, and so we call it an illusion: an appearance
taken to be real. In theatrical drama, appearance and reality are
not mere themes, but essentials. When we begin to see reality
itself in theatrical terms, we recognize that "illusion is only a specifically theatrical term for a process inherent in all social interaction" (Burns 17).

What we see in drama is not so much action as interaction.
And interaction is shown best through that particular kind of lan-

guage use called dialogue—words and word-users in close inter-action. Language is a kind of action. Dramatic theory has seen theatre too much as a composition of words rather than of activi-ties (Styan 109); in drama, language *is* action, and action is lan-guage. "One could go further and claim that all language in drama of necessity *becomes* action. In drama we are concerned not only with *what* a character says—the purely semantic mean-ing of their words—but with what the character *does* with his words" (Esslin 40).

Speech-act linguists elaborate the idea of doing things with words in a terminology too technical for our teaching:

> If language is to register within the physical context of the stage and come into contact with bodies and objects thereon, it must participate in the deictic ostension of which gesture is the prime vehicle. (Elam 73)

> In a play, the action rides on a train of illocutions . . . move-ments within the social world of the play appear most clearly in their illocutionary acts. (Ohmann, qtd. in Elam 159)

But rough translations of these terms can be helpful. Ostension means showing—words show as well as tell; deixis means point-ing—words point to the people using them and to the circum-stances within which they are spoken. Words are illocutionary when they perform an act in being said: questioning, command-ing, promising, asserting. Words in dramatic dialogue are un-usually active in the ways they show, point, and perform. The most suggestive term is *performative:* a play is a performance where words perform. Words are only part of what characters do in interacting: "dramatic meaning cannot lie in words alone, but in voices and the tone of voices, in the pace of the speaking and the silences between; and not alone in this, but also in the ges-ture and expression of the actor, the physical distinctions be-tween him and others . . ." (Styan 26). A good introduction to the performative nature of dialogue is through what Kathleen George (17–18) calls "an open scene," a fragmentary script with-out context.

1.	Oh	1.	Listen
2.	Yes	2.	No
1.	Why are you doing this	1.	So different
2.	It's the best thing	2.	Not really
1.	You can't mean it	1.	Oh
2.	No, I'm serious	2.	You're quite good
1.	Please	1.	Forget it
2.	What	2.	What
1.	What does this mean	1.	Go
2.	Nothing	2.	I will

"In an art form in which the structuring of the work in a time dimension is of such importance, it is only natural that timing, a sense of timing, is the essential hallmark of the good playwright, as well as of director and actor" (Esslin 51). Time is an obsessive theme of *Our Town* and a complex problem of *Othello*. Time is a special condition of any play. Time in a novel is fluid and ambiguous; a play is acted out here and now as we watch, and it takes a certain segment of real time to perform. Yet, time is also illusionary, make-believe. What happens in present time may be set in some other time, no time, all times. Theatre compresses time into dramatic time. A fifteen-minute scene may pretend to "cover" an hour. Scenes that happen "at the same time" must be seen in sequence. More than one time-sequence may be going on "at the same time." Elam's scheme is simple enough: (1) actual performance time (duration); (2) the present time of the action; (3) plot time, in which actions are performed; (4) chronological time of the story; (5) historical time in which the play is supposed to take place. Whatever version we adopt for teaching, the point is that time in theatrical drama is *different* and *multiple*, and we are affected accordingly.

One major effect is suggested by Esslin (28), and our example *Our Town* serves as well as his: in each performance, Hamlet is present and goes through the sequence of the events that happened to him as if they were happening now for the first time. The same is true of ritual. To teach drama, we must communicate an understanding of ritual and related concepts: ceremony, play, game, routine. "One can," suggests Esslin, "look at drama as a manifestation of the *play instinct:* children playing mother and father or cowboys and Indians are, in some sense, improvising drama. Or one can see drama as a manifestation of one of humanity's prime social needs, that of *ritual:* tribal dances, religious services, great state occasions all contain strong dramatic elements" (10). A play is governed by the rules of a game, and ritual is the name of the game (Styan 237). The pretend reality of game or play and the other reality of ritual or ceremony are just two levels of the same spectacle.

Ritual or ceremony is a set of actions that happen repeatedly, predictably, and in accordance with certain prescribed rules as to what is appropriate: language is formal; gesture is stylized and expressive; actions *say* things as much as *do* things (consider the handshake). They are performed. A ritual or ceremony performs actions as important, meaningful; and symbolic props are often used (flags, crosses, wine, even ice cream sodas). Ritual and routine are different but connected. The breakfasts in *Our Town* are routinized, but are they ritualized? My wife and I bring coffee to share in bed every morning; we treat this routine as a ritual. The kind of ritual called a ceremony is a public occasion serving social functions. People participate by playing set roles; roles transcend personalities. Even the spectator has a role to play. The spectators witness the ceremony and transmit signals back to the performers. A play is a social event in which all participants have roles to play. One who sees his role in life to be that of spectator, fool, hero, or whatever, is viewing life in terms of its theatricality.

With the concept of role-playing, we reach the idea of character, of playing a character or role. This idea may be misunderstood by faulty analogy with character in story. We have characters in drama only because we have actors first: "It is the condition of drama that it needs human agents, the actors," says Styan (157). "A character," as Stanislavsky defined it, "is a new human being born of the elements of the actor himself united with those of the character conceived by the author of the play" (Styan 149). Character in a play is character as performed by an actor. "In performance there is constant interaction between the actor's real personality and his role" (Styan 145). There is also tension which the spectator cannot help but witness: the actor is a real person whose role is to impersonate a fiction, to create an illusion, to impose a character on the audience. He is literally a player, an impersonator, one who works a confidence trick with the complicity of the audience. As Burns says, "The dangerous qualities inherent in acting are those qualities inherent in human nature, deceit, irreverent mimicry and the power to arouse in others passions and emotions normally controlled" (151).

The play is made up of role-play and role interaction. The performing of roles is not merely a theme of some plays; it is a necessary condition of all plays. In life, we play roles all the time. The relation among our several roles, and between our roles and what we think we really are, is problematic. The roles we play seem to belong not to us but to our actions and social situations; I am not always "in character" as teacher, and my students are not always students. Our roles constrain us, sometimes belie us, make us feel we are impersonating ourselves. (Such is the theme of one influential contemporary school of social psychology.) And yet, without our several roles we may feel without identity.

The problem is central to *Our Town*, and this is part of what makes it a *play*. The performers of *Our Town* interact in their roles: father/mother/son/daughter; husband/wife; newsboy/milk-man/doctor/editor—"all those terribly important things" that fade as the "eternal part" comes out (52). Gestures, actions, props, all serve to mark the roles they play. The fact that the props are imaginary, the gestures merely mimed, serves to emphasize their typicality, to foreground them as role behavior, ritual gesture. George and Emily resist their new roles; Doc Gibbs finds it difficult to play the father, and Editor Webb finds it difficult to play the father-in-law. But out of role is out of play. When Emily returns from the dead, she must reassume roles no longer hers and watch herself do so. She seeks to force others out of their roles but cannot. The only comfortable role player is the Stage Manager. He feels no uneasiness in shifting roles: stage hand, house director, philosopher, timekeeper, druggist, minister. He is master of ceremonies. He knows what is important.

And with that most important word, we tackle theme. A theme in a play, says Burns, is "a sequence of acts, interpretations and responses reinterpreted as a whole, by the spectator" (218). In *Our Town*, the entire sequence turns on that question, What is really important? Are the "smallest events in our daily life" really important? "In ordinary life, ceremony serves the purpose of distinguishing an important event or of endowing an ordinary event with dignity or mystery" (Burns 212). In the theatre, stage and staging themselves have the effect of signifying importance. An image most compelling for me (since I saw it first many years ago) is the one Max Frisch recalls of an early arrival for rehearsal at a Zurich theatre. An empty stage; a dark or half-lit auditorium.

> Suddenly the lights on the stage went up, a stage-hand appeared and placed some chairs in readiness for the rehearsal that was about to start. Frisch describes how he watched this activity with rapt attention, how suddenly every movement of the man acquired tremendous significance, simply because it was happening on a lit stage, within the picture frame of that stage. For we are conditioned to think of a stage (or a television or cinema screen) as spaces within which significant things are being shown; they therefore concentrate our attention and compel us to try and arrange everything that happens there into a significant pattern, to make sense of it as a pattern. (Esslin 52)

In theatre, everything signifies. The actor interprets—performs the meaning of—the author's script. The audience interprets this interpretation. To understand theatrical drama is to be able to participate in this interpretive complex.

But how, if at all, can we hope to achieve this kind of understanding in students sitting in a classroom? Recall the essayists in *Teaching Shakespeare*. For them, there seems a dispute over what to do about "the specifically theatrical aspect, the performability, of Shakespeare's texts" (xii).

> The teacher of literature should be warned that to conceive of drama as performance may mean to shift his fundamental

assumptions about the stability and integrity of the literary text. . . .

Performance is within the province of teachers of literature who recognize that the kinds of decisions they make as literary critics are involved in every theatrical production. . . .

A classroom is not a theatre, and teachers who aspire to be actors should remember Holofernes' fallen countenance [see *Love's Labour's Lost;* we have already been told that Holofernes is "the only memorable teacher in Shakespeare's plays," and that he is "a vain and dogmatic pedant"]. (Edens xiii)

To see what's amiss here, let's move backwards. First, Holofernes is not the only memorable teacher. To think so is to take a particularly narrow view of what teaching is. Second, the classroom *is* a theatre. To think not is to take an equally narrow view of what a theatre is. Of course performance is within our province, for performance is part of what is done in a classroom. Third, it seems curious to "warn" teachers about conceiving of drama as performance. What else can it be? And those "fundamental assumptions about the stability and integrity of the literary text": is a Shakespeare text now so established? Have not such assumptions been undermined with regard to all kinds of texts? Finally, this "specifically theatrical aspect" or "performability": is there any other aspect, or if there are others, can they be separated from it?

It is easy to understand what these writers would avoid: to substitute acting Shakespeare for studying him; to substitute the seeing of performances for the study of them; to turn students into inept amateur actors; to treat plays only in terms of "stagecraft." I fully agree that "the availability of oral or visual examples of the text in itself does not assure a critical understanding. It is the way the examples are used and the critical apparatus brought to bear that counts" (Beckerman in Edens 314). Carroll gives us the key: "the idea of performance, not performance as such, has place in the classroom" (60). The point is that we must teach how to imagine performance. Our problem is not how to balance text and performance, but how to teach reading as a process of imagining and interpreting performance.

We can be guided by a simple question: Who alone reads a whole play in this way? Who performs what Tyrone Guthrie calls "the one really creative function . . . which is to be at rehearsal a highly receptive, highly concentrated, highly critical sounding-board for the performance, an audience of one" (Burns 84), the function of "editing and coordinating the multiplicity of selves realized by individual actors and, above all, defining the tone of the whole action" (Burns 171)? Who is "the man who interprets" (Burns 173)? The director studies a play in terms of the *idea* of performance. The idea of *the director as reader* is, however unrealizable, the ideal we should strive for. We ask students not how they would perform the climactic scene of *Our Town*, Emily's return, but rather how they would plan it, direct it, for performance. To do this is to *interpret* the scene in all its theatricality, and to interpret it in terms of the play as a whole.

The scene of Emily's return has been, for me, one of the strangest and saddest, and one of the most perfectly theatrical, I have ever known, since, in 1939, I watched repeatedly from backstage (I played both newsboys; Wilder himself played Stage Manager) while Martha Scott rehearsed and performed it. Few scenes show more vividly how gesture, movement, and position are inseparable from words, and how words indicate gesture, movement, position.

Consider what Emily is doing. She is trying to repossess persons, places, interactions, things. She yearns toward them, wants to touch them, is repulsed by them as they shut her out. We must see a physical rhythm of attraction and retreat, entry and withdrawal. She must be in the scene and yet out of it, play within its illusory spaces and yet ignore them. She has a dual role: the dead Emily returning, the child Emily on her birthday. She must watch herself playing it. She has usurped the role of spectator. We do not just watch as Howie and Mr. Webb, the constable, Joe, and Mrs. Webb repeat their timeless routines (rituals?); we must watch her watch them as she watches herself. The scene is intensely real to her, and yet it is an illusion; the Stage Manager has staged it for her. Prospero that he is, he can produce any scene she chooses, and the actors will obey his commands. But that is the point: they are just actors in life as in play; they do not *realize* life but simply play it. She tries to realize it, but can only look on.

The theme of her anguish is that no one really looks. The painful climax comes when she realizes that no one has time really to look at one another. The actors must carefully *not* look at each other as we watch her watching; we must feel the infinite distance between her/us and them. Movement, gesture, spatial interaction—all signify what she discovers: the living are literally *blind* people. Emily at last *sees* things when they are no longer there. The dead sit quietly, with eternal time to see, to watch. We too are dead.

Within this context, we can imagine and discuss how her lines could be "read," seeing that they must express in alternation, in tension, wonder and grief, anguish and delight, longing and repulsion. None of us would be capable of acting them out in class, but together we can explore what their performance means. And from the vantage point of this scene we can look back over the play as a whole, its rhythms, its form, its theme.

IV

With our "middle" play, teaching has concentrated on the elements of drama as form and on the director as ideal reader. But of course, the director must also read his audience. As we turn to the unique challenges of teaching a Shakespeare play, we will gradually shift our attention from director to audience. The historical and cultural context of a play is embodied in its implied audience. Without this context, we cannot understand the forms of a Shakespeare play. But first we must carry our teaching through the earlier stages, using the early acts to do so. As will be seen in this plan for several sessions, the matter of context arises late in the plan, with the question of motivation.

1. A showing of *Othello*, act 1 (film or videotape). Getting accustomed to the play as seen and heard, to appearances, voices, gestures, to reading the text for performance clues.

2. An open-ended class exploration of lying and honesty, their forms and variations, their rights and wrongs, carried on in connection with reading act 2.

3. Words as actions; the powers of words. A close study of the major dialogues of act 3, and the verbal and gestural interactions of Othello and Iago. Alternative readings of specific exchanges, with taped performance variants for comparison.

4. Character and role in performance. Directing specific scenes in act 4; discussing different ideas of performance and performability.

5. Motivation and its meanings in drama; a review of acts 1 through 4, with an emphasis on the problem of Iago.

6. Summary synthesis of form in the play as a whole; the significances of place and time; story, plot, and rhythm.

7. Othello's end and the ends of tragedy: mode, impact, tragic meaning. (If time allows and the means are available, see the entire play.)

The first two parts of this scheme are intended to provide a predisciplinary or "romance" exploration (as with our teaching of *She Stoops*). Parts three and four follow the more precise and analytical mode of the *Our Town* pedagogy. There is no need to spell them out in detail. But even at these earlier stages, we can begin to sense two major theatrical features of Shakespeare's historical world, and these will finally be understood only through contextual guidance. One is the unusual ambiguity of appearance in a world so dependent on public ceremonial. Seeing parts of the play and planning their performance, we recognize how many scenes take place in the dark or near-dark, and thus how delusive is a dependence (Othello's obsession with being shown) on ocular proof. The other, also obvious in performance, is the significant fear of disorder. All kinds and levels of disorder correspond.

Once students discover what special force appearance, disorder, and correspondence have here, they will be better equipped to understand a Shakespearian form. Once they begin to understand this, we can take the next step and suggest how this form reflects the way the author perceived the world in which he lived.

The step occurs with part five on the plan. The popular question of motivation arises and with it the problem of Iago. I have postponed it in an effort to recognize that motivation may have special meanings in a play. Iago is not a character in a novel; he is a player, an actor, who exists in and for his actions—some would say he has no existence outside of his roles. We must consider how he plays his roles. The range of performable Iagos permitted by the text is wide, and different performers portray Iago differently. Motivation in a play is a major part of the play's meaning. We cannot think about what motivates Iago without thinking about what motivates everyone in this play: why Desdemona and Othello love each other; why Roderigo persists as Iago's gull; why Venice elects Othello commander; why Cassio falls so easily into disgrace; why Othello so easily loses faith; why Desdemona alone is impervious to Iago's powers of deception. The play itself repeatedly confronts the question of why Iago acts as he does; he himself often speaks of it. So we cannot evade the question even if we find no consistent or sufficient answer.

In teaching, we have to concede that there are problems to which we will find no full solutions. A solution depends on one's comprehensive point of view, and such a point of view is what our ideal reader, the director, reads to acquire. He cannot acquire it, however, merely from the play itself. He must make assumptions about the play's real context, its audience. We as audience understand Iago's motives according to our own beliefs about human nature—a good discussion should force us to realize this. Shakespeare had his own audience with its own beliefs, and he made his play with that audience in mind. We need historical context.

Consider (possibly in our course) the approaches to Iago summarized by Stanley Hyman. (1) *Generic:* Iago is a stage villain who delights in wickedness. (But what was Shakespeare's audience's idea of the stage villain?) (2) *Theological:* Iago is a devil or diabolist. (What was their idea of the devil?) (3) *Aesthetic:* Iago is an artist, an ominous caricature of the playwright. (What was their idea of the artist?) (4) *Psychoanalytic:* Iago, a latent homosexual, is disgusted by heterosexual love. (What were their ideas of sexuality?) (5) *Ideological:* Iago is a Machiavelli, a power-mad egoist. (What were their ideas of power?) For Hyman, the theological takes top place, and it demands historical perspective. Shakespeare's audience could believe in diabolism; our students may not. But with probing, they may well discover their own secular versions, and thus find more access to the context of *Othello*.

Finally (part seven of our plan), we reach the end and the ends of tragedy, the mode of *Othello*. What makes us respond as we do? Once again, we study ourselves as an audience, but in doing so, we also recall Shakespeare's. Do our ideas of the tragic differ from theirs? It is a historical question, and we need to answer it if we would have the contexts for understanding this play, or any play. It brings us as close as we can get to the maker himself, prepares the way for a whole course in Shakespeare the author. And that is a course of a different color.

NINE

Performing to Strangers

I

In our culture at least, learning is largely personal. Students, like other people, learn from persons. When they begin to conceive of authors as persons, their reading becomes more personal. This may help to explain why they flock to courses with titles like Shakespeare or Dickens, Twain or Joyce, Austen and Eliot, Fitzgerald and Hemingway. What is special about teaching an author? I will assume that our author is a novelist, and that we have several weeks to consider four texts. I will use Jane Austen as an example.

The case is special, of course. The author's preferred form must make a difference in the very nature of authorship. The author's choice of genre is conditioned by the cultural moment and the state of the genre, and these conditions interplay with personal priorities. The case is special, too, in that Austen was a woman author in an institutional literature governed by male writers and male assumptions, one of which held the novel to be peculiarly a woman's form. But for all these variables, the fundamental pedagogical issues and options are largely the same. What are the curricular options? Teachers of authors probably stand at various points on a spectrum. Their courses range from the extreme of "We will simply read the works attributed to a certain author" all the way to "We will study the author's writings in an effort to discover a psychobiographical portrait of the author, a

life-myth, a personal figure under the carpet." The middle range
is occupied by Scholes, for example, in teaching Hemingway:

> I am going to argue . . . that all three passages, taken to-
> gether reveal a pattern or paradigm that is a persistent fea-
> ture of the subjectivity we call "Ernest Hemingway." It is
> this very kind of persistence, in fact, which is the principal
> external evidence for that subjective continuity we recognize
> as the "same" human being. (50)

Which option will we choose? Before choosing, we need to understand what idea of author we endorse.

In some current theory we find ominous reports of the Death
of the Author. As with the deaths of Nietzsche's God and Clemens's
Mark Twain, the reports are exaggerated. But exaggerated or
not, they are useful, for they provoke us to ask what we do when
we teach an author, what concept of author shapes our teaching.
The New Critical orthodoxy and the Newer Criticism that would
replace it share one dogma: in the reading of a literary text, the
biographical author should be irrelevant. She is "extrinsic," said
the New Critics; "extratextual," say the newer ones. This extratextual person has no authority over the text. Trust the tale, not
the teller, said Frost; what matters of me, said Faulkner, is in my
books. Rhetorical critics, less extreme, have warned us to distinguish between such entities as "persona," "implied author," and
"real author," the third of these, like a Trinitarian God, absent,
remote, or hidden.

The reasons for such a dogma may be philosophical, method-
ological, or even political. Whatever the reasons, we now distinguish between two different concepts of Author.

A rather melodramatic statement by Barthes (in *The Pleasure
of the Text*) leads the way:

> lost in the midst of the text (not *behind* it, like a *deus ex ma-
> china*) [or, we might say, not outside like a patriarch pulling
> the strings] . . . there is always the other, the author. As in-
> stitution, the author is dead: his civil status, his biographical
> person have disappeared; dispossessed, they no longer exer-

cise over his work the formidable paternity whose account literary history, teaching, and public opinion had the responsibility of establishing and renewing. . . . But in the text, in a way, I *desire* the author: I need his figure (which is neither his representation nor his projection) as he needs mine . . . (27)

That is, as an implicated companion in the making of meanings. Elsewhere, Barthes calls that older idea of the author a "somewhat decrepit deity of the old criticism" and would deny the deity his status as "the subject, the impulse, the authority, the Father, whence his work would proceed" (S/Z 211).

If (so goes the argument) we grant the author such authority, we not only abdicate our roles as readers. We delude ourselves as to the actual relation of author to text. Jane Austen, like many authors, spoke of her novels as her children, and so they were. But like other prudent parents (mothers, at least?), she also knew the limits and flaws in her power to control and maintain. One cannot know a child simply as projection of the begetter. One can know the Father/Mother only in the Child. Barthes might mock such theological analogies, but they are operative.

If, then, we do not teach the author as original and external authority, What is an Author? There is a useful, if puzzling, essay so titled by Michel Foucault. For the older idea, Foucault would substitute an authorial presence or "function" in the text. The text did have a responsible begetter and originated in a personal design. But this author is known to us readers only as a construct we make out of our own operations: "the connections that we make, the traits that we establish as pertinent, the continuities that we recognize, or the exclusions that we practice" (Foucault 110). The construct we make may not be unitary, but instead plural. We may find a plurality of Austens.

This is not really so shocking. We know already that, in the process of writing, an author is related to her creation in three ways. She is the originating impulse. She is also the giver of form. She is also the speaker of language. In the actual process, the relations change. The original impulse or design is altered in the forming, and the speaking manifests and modifies both. Various operations and voices "speak for" the author, but these spokespersons shift in reliability and distance. If this is all that is meant by the Death of the Author, perhaps we and the author can survive it. Perhaps the newer idea is closer to the way we read anyway.

But one thing intrinsic to reading the works of an author gradually forces itself on our attention. The further we go, the more influenced our reading is by certain formative expectations, and these we identify with an implied author, a "second self," an "official scribe." Wayne Booth is right: "However impersonal [the author] may try to be, his reader will inevitably construct a picture of this official scribe" (qtd. in Chatman 148). And such a picture provokes a certain kind of question. "A poet," wrote George Gordon, "is a man who throws a stone through your window and you pursue him down the street because you want to know something more than the stone" (9). Our question is, Why stones? Why throw? Why be an author, write texts, write this text? Why, from her twelfth year (1787–88) to her death in 1817, did Jane Austen increasingly find her chief social role, her life vocation, in writing a certain kind of novel, refusing all others? Will the author in the text provide any answers?

II

Not easily. Austen has proven unusually enigmatic. Virginia Woolf felt that "of all great writers she is the most difficult to catch in the act of greatness" (Watt 15n). "In one way," says John Bayley, "we know her too well . . . and in another way we do not know her at all" (1–2). An essential disclosure of her novels is the impossibility of ever fully knowing another person. Social knowledge is always problematic and variable. The problem of social knowledge in the novel has a history.

Some historians of the novel find its genesis in a secularizing of theological individualism, or in the origins of psychology—ethical and empirical individualism. Others emphasize the growth of scientific interest in society. The novel, says Arendt, established itself as "the only entirely social art form" with the rise of the "social" (38–39). Society was coming to be seen as *the world*. When a novelist portrayed a young individual entering the world, she showed a frightening, all-encompassing sphere of deceptive pressures and illusions, but also of fortune and status—a place called Society. Only here could the individual undergo testing for a secure and meaningful place, what Austen called an "establishment."

The establishment of the novel during Austen's lifetime is also associated with the coming to social power of a wealthy, leisured bourgeoisie. Here, the novel found its growing readership, a large proportion women; the novel's social establishment was a significant event in women's social and psychological history. The novel centered on domestic intimacies and entrapments, on the intensities of private life, at a time when the legal idea of privacy and the modern ideal of privacy as an urgent need and value were coming to the fore—perhaps in response to the rise of the "social." The novel's peculiar tensions of social world and private self may be the key to its formal genesis and lasting appeal. Ride the subway today, emblem of the social with its crowding anonymity, and watch the solitary readers hidden in bulging paperback novels, counter-societies of the imagination where interpersonal knowledge and feeling flourish, intimacies are shared, and the social is secretly eluded. What Gilbert and Gubar say of Austen has broad application:

> Authorship for Austen is an escape from the very restraints she imposes on her female characters. And in this respect she seems typical, for women may have contributed so significantly to narrative fiction precisely because it effectively objectifies, even as it sustains and hides, the subjectivity of the author. (168)

No wonder such an author may seem too well known and yet not known at all.

The form had the same strange appeal to some male authors. The private and compensatory social worlds of Walter Scott were created at the same time as Austen's. The most vivid description of the novel in such terms comes not from a woman, but from Rousseau, recalling the genesis of *La Nouvelle Heloise:*

[S]eeing nothing that existed worthy of my exalted feelings, I fostered them in an ideal world which my creative imagination soon peopled with beings after my own heart . . . I created for myself societies of perfect creatures celestial in their virtue and in their beauty, and of reliable, tender, and faithful friends such as I had never found here below (398) . . . I imagined two women friends, rather than two of my own sex, since although examples of such friendship are rarer they are also more beautiful. (400)

In such worlds, the failures of social knowledge and feeling, the deceits of social roles, the disjunctions of private and social can be given meaningful forms. Georg Lukacs might have been glossing Rousseau's passage when he wrote that "the irony of the novel is the self-correction of the world's fragility: inadequate relations can transform themselves into a fanciful yet well-ordered round of misunderstandings and cross-purposes, within which everything is seen as many-sided, within which things appear as isolated and yet connected" (75). Is this why our students read novels? We should ask them.

The inner form of the novel, Lukacs argues, begins with the dissonance of the ideal and the real and embodies an ironic view of it. All prose fiction, in Trilling's well-known statement, "is a variation on the theme of *Don Quixote*. . . . the shifting and conflict of social classes becomes the field of the problem of knowledge, of how we know and of how reliable our knowledge is" ("Manners" 57–58). Such is the history of Austen's central problem.

I begin my teaching with *Emma*. Author studies normally proceed in a chronological line, on assumptions—often unexamined—about development. We should test the meanings of that crucial idea, but they are better tested if we do not assume them a priori in our teaching order. I begin by acknowledging the oft-claimed maturity of *Emma* (no developmental inquiry can truly begin anywhere but with maturity), then move back to *Pride and Prejudice*, jump forwards to *Persuasion*, stop to introduce materials and issues of biographical context, and return fi-

nally to *Emma* for a *second reading*. This finale rests on two assumptions: (1) the second reading is a better test of reading
Austen (or perhaps any author); (2) the second reading comes
to focus more sharply on questions of authorial identity and
achievement. The time for repeating is amply justified.

We begin with the text of *Emma* and the problem as formulated by Lukacs and Trilling. But we begin also with the logistical
problems of teaching any large novel. Necessity can mother advantages. Class discussion must begin when students have read
only a few chapters for the first time. We can explore the conditions of getting into the text, into this social world. We can question the nature of the novel's largeness and its smallness, and ask
how the amplitude and the leisurely pace affect us and justify
themselves. The process of social knowledge—for us, for the
characters—must move in its own way. We discover only that our
interest is focused on one central figure in a small group, whom
we come to know only gradually. We trace the process whereby
the text creates, segment by segment, a social world whose texture or atmosphere envelops us. We watch the emerging relationship of person, world, and reader, and see that it is problematic, *the* problem.

Is Ortega's imperative carried out?

> The author must see to it that the reader is cut off from his
> real horizon and imprisoned in a small, hermetically sealed
> universe—the inner realm of the novel. He must make a
> "villager" of him and interest him in the inhabitants of this
> realm . . . To turn each reader into a temporary "provincial"
> is the great secret of the novelist. (83)

The process is at once private and social. The language gradually
builds an image in and of the reader's mind, so that he feels "in"
the society and privately possessed of it. Some readers have
found the experience especially "inward" with *Emma*. In *Emma*,
Mudrick believes, "the author is in her novel and never out of
it . . . no other of Jane Austen's novels offers so pleasant and comfortable an atmosphere" (qtd. in Halperin 268). Brown claims
that *Emma*'s

first great strength lies in the ability to draw the reader in. We are made happy in the traps that are laid for us; we roll in the nets and sleep . . . the pleasure comes from our willing immersion in the everyday concerns and relationships of this world . . . The novel's very self-absorption makes it acceptable and wonderful. It is a world that believes in itself entirely, and hypnotized, we too believe. (101)

Whoa! Where does Brown's "we" come from? What of the students who don't experience this, who say (think), "I can't get into it," and perhaps stop reading? We teachers must not imply that they simply don't know how to read or don't like Austen. Rather, in class we should explore what keeps them "out" as well as what draws others "in." Some will agree with Brown; others may agree with Trilling: "*Emma* is a very difficult novel . . . the difficulty of *Emma* is never overcome" (Intro. to *Emma* viii). Can both be right? Of course. Brown's own language is strikingly ambivalent: "traps," "self-absorption," "entire belief," "hypnosis"— all suggest distance and disapproval. The test of the mature Austen reader (the end of our course?) will be to sustain the perilous balance she requires between in and out, immersion and rejection, sympathy and judgment. Why does she require this? This question engages us with the "author"—but not yet.

We should concede early on that the limits and complacencies of Austen's world disturb some, and should not merely repeat the special pleading (though we may agree) that the limits simply prove her fine artistic prudence. We should not simply declare hers a conservative nature with conservative values—at least not until we understand. Some feel that Austen created her social world simply in order to castigate it: "sometimes it seems" to Virginia Woolf "as if her creatures were born merely to give Jane Austen the supreme delight of slicing their heads off" (Watt 20). But it is too early to conjecture about authorial motive. Here, in first reading (our romance stage), we are merely trying to work out our own first relations with this world.

It is not easy. This Emma is not easy to know, like, judge. The biographical author anticipated this, calling her "a heroine whom no one but myself will much like," and the other character who knows her best, Knightley, says in chapter 5: "There is an anxiety, a curiosity in what one feels for Emma. I wonder what will become of her!" Much about her world (not really "hers," though she would make it so) is not comfortable. Her relations with it are vitiated by egoism, snobbery, fantasy, manipulative power. But these are what Austen called "first impressions," and if we rely on them we fall into the very traps of which Austen made fiction. Reader beware! The book's meaning and the conditions of knowing it are the same. "The book," writes Trilling, "is like a person—not to be comprehended fully and finally by any other person" (Intro. ix).

But why in this social world is interpersonal knowledge so uncertain? This is the question that opens our second discussion. Why is Emma so ludicrously, painfully, mistaken about Elton and Harriet? Are the causes remedied or remediable? Why so mistaken (pitiably? ludicrously?) about Frank and Jane? Were the mistakes preventable? How well does Emma know her father, Miss Bates, Mrs. Elton, the Coleses, and others, and how does her knowing condition our knowing and feeling about her? How do our knowledge and feeling alter as we discover the role she plays (must play?) in the Frank-Jane mystery? Are there connections between knowing and feeling? Between knowing others and knowing oneself?

These questions raise a central question of the book's method. The book carries us mostly with only Emma's faulty consciousness to guide us. Concealment has been severely criticized, yet we have been made victims of it. The author has rejected two options: Emma does not tell her own story; the story is not told by someone who tells what Emma cannot know. Choose any episode. Retell it as if by Emma, and then as if by someone who conceals nothing. Are there reasons for the book's method? Are they sufficient?

By this time in our classes, we can look back and see the book's patterning and sequencing. The rhythms of arrival and departure focus and refocus on several social groupings. Others are excluded. Think back to your first impressions of this world. We never see the life of the Martins, or of the poor. We never visit Emma's sister in London, the Bath of Mrs. Elton, the Ireland of the Dixons and Campbells, the Churchills' estate. Have your views of this exclusiveness altered? Has your relation to this world changed?

Here ends our first reading of *Emma*. The author remains to be found.

III

We turn back next to *Pride and Prejudice* (*PP*), and assign the first dozen chapters (fifty pages or so). With *PP*, I want to play two radically different pedagogical roles. At the start, I will play the discreet clerk-chair and listen. Then I will play the critic, suggesting problems with this Popular Classic (it can easily survive my challenge). Here is an initial agenda. It takes a cautious, awkward first step toward authorial presence or function, opens the "motive" can of worms, and bows briefly to issues of assessment.

In these early chapters, what signs are there of the "Author of *Emma*"? Having listed some, can we connect them meaningfully? What noteworthy differences? Can we invent any explanations for why the books were made to be different? Do these explanations refer to a biographical author's age, development, maturity of art and outlook, circumstances?

I have no idea what I will hear in response, but some replies are not hard to anticipate. Socioeconomic world and its limits, problems, values seem similar: domesticity, small town, preoccupation with status and social behavior, marriage, matchmaking, money; a heroine of intelligence, independence, pride; a few simple-minded fools and some deceivers; misunderstandings and misjudgments. A few students will sense similarities of style. Other replies are harder to anticipate. Why does such a world find its central institution in marriage? Why, given this marital obsession, are misunderstandings so common and momentous? Why do such happenings turn on the experience (inexperience) of this kind of heroine? And why, in the face of such errors and anxieties, do we readers feel so amused and entertained?

What differences will be noticed? The question calls for descriptive answers, but I expect relative assessments to mix in. Perhaps we should acknowledge a fact of critical tradition. *PP* has long held its place as Austen's most popular, widely enjoyed novel. How might we account for the greater popularity of *PP*? Two possibilities might be discussed. *PP* is the livelier, funnier book, livelier in its behavior, funnier in its fools and wits? *PP* is the simpler book, less elusive in its goings-on, more explicit in its judgments? *PP* might be called more comic and more satiric? If so, aren't our relations as readers to the texts different? Don't we sense a different relation of author to text, author to us? We do *not* experience (do we?) what Brown thought we experienced with *Emma*—immersion, contented entrapment. We are outsiders, onlookers, distanced in critical amusement. Why? For one reason, the novel in its earlier chapters is much more scenic, more like dramatic performance. The characters seem to be performing. Why, since Elizabeth performs so well, so wittily, and appears so to relish the performances of others, does Darcy advise her (in chapter 31), "We neither of us perform to strangers"? What compels people to perform in public? Is this less true in Emma's world?

We are exploring how our relations as reader to text differ. What about the relations of heroine to world, author to world, author to heroine? The status of the heroine, and thus of the author, seems easy to misunderstand. Numerous readers jump to Mudrick's conclusion: in *PP*, "Jane Austen allows her heroine to share her own characteristic response to the world" (388–89). But how did Mudrick become so sure of the characteristic response of "Austen"? Elizabeth is often taken as Austen surrogate or spokesperson; she sounds so much like the narrator, who is supposed to be Austen, that they are identical.

But if we assume this identity of response between author and heroine, how must we feel when Elizabeth is punished for being cruelly prejudicial? Is what we feel when Elizabeth feels shame different from what we feel when Emma's conscience troubles her? And what do we say to the claim of Gilbert and Gubar that Austen "can reprove as indecent in a heroine what is necessary to an author" (168)? We may admire Elizabeth for her principled disapproval of Charlotte, but what then do we make (chapter 24) of a principled person for whom "there are few people whom I really love, and still fewer of whom I think well. The more I see of the world, the more I am dissatisfied with it"? Sister Jane warns, "Do not give way to such feelings as these. They will ruin your happiness." We will review such statements later when the sight of Pemberley confirms Elizabeth's love for its wealthy master. Has Elizabeth grown happy and loving by becoming less principled? Have there been alterations in Elizabeth's mode of response, or in ours, or even (shocking possibility) in the author's? If characters and readers change, why should an author not change? If this happens, if shifts or inconsistencies result, must we judge the book as flawed, the author as unreliable or irresponsible? I have assumed my exaggerated second pedagogical stance, and am challenging the book's unity. I am doing so, first, to question the notion of a classic as a closed repository of fixed meanings, and, second, to encourage a different way of reading. Two manageable essays would help, and I assign them: D. W. Harding's "Regulated Hatred" and John Bayley's "The 'Irresponsibility' of Jane Austen." My aim is not to insert "authorities" into our discussions, and not to debate their particular interpretations. Rather, they provide two different ways of defining the author's relations to her work and our relations to the author.

Harding's hypothesis is that there are two conflicting ways of reading an Austen novel and two kinds of readers. The conventional readers (my grandmother was one) turn to Austen for innocent fun and tranquil escape. To them she offers "rather exaggerated figures of fun" to be enjoyed and tolerated. But the "real Austen" (Harding's reality construct) carefully conceals herself from such readers. Harding's "real Austen" is disclosed only to sharp-eyed readers who catch clues. She "detests and fears" the "monsters" she caricatures, and is desperately seeking "some mode of existence," some way of sharing the "only available social world," while protecting her own "spiritual survival" (Watt 170–71). Bayley's hypothesis is more optimistic and liberal. He assumes a single readership, for whom there is "a real questioning or wondering, an apparent dialogue between our own intelligence and another's." A "peculiarly immediate and yet equivocal attitude" in Austen "challenges and fascinates us" (1–3). (It may in fact puzzle the hell out of students who have been taught that equivocal attitudes don't occur in authors of classic texts.) In successive readings, thinks Bayley, we discover new significances, changes in perspective of "our own world in relation to hers." But this is not concealment or duplicity; rather, it is her willingness to grant her subject and reader a degree of freedom to form their own impressions and judgments.

If Harding and Bayley are correct, the typical assessment of *PP* as classic cannot be just: the developing novel gradually and coherently qualifies Elizabeth's mode of response, educates her to the dangers of her behavior (the recklessness of Lydia, the cynicism of her father), and shows her and us that her independence need not be surrendered but only regulated. But we need not resolve the issue among these three to find useful the questions they raise for student, author, world. How much authority can such divergent critics have over the student? How much authority should the author have over the reader? How much can it be withheld without irresponsibility, and is authorial duplicity tolerable in a classic text? Analogous problems confront Elizabeth's social world. To be overly submissive to authority is as mistaken as to be overly resistant. To fail to influence or persuade may be irresponsible (as in Mr. Bennett). When should authority be exercised, and when withheld?

These, of course, are the cruxes that give title to our third novel, *Persuasion*, where they share center stage with our earlier questions about social knowledge.

IV

I have space here only to offer a sequence of questions. In monitoring answers, I will adopt yet another pedagogical stance, the Romantic position that *Persuasion* is fundamentally different and reveals an "Austen" essentially changed.

1. We now have many expectations about an "Austen novel." As we read together, let's describe and discuss how they play against our perceptions. Focus on changes, noticing that change itself is one of the novel's chief themes. Is this an "Austen novel"?

2. Take the social world, remembering the worlds of *Emma* and *PP*. Has it changed? Try to relate this revised construct of social world to our initial problem in Austen: knowing, judging, communicating with others. Has it changed in nature or cause?

3. How do our answers connect with the problem suggested by the novel's title, *Persuasion*? To be persuaded is to be sure of one's knowledge and feelings? To communicate feelings and judgments to others is to risk persuading them? When is persuasion desirable, when dangerous, when both?

4. Our knowing and feeling as readers depend in part on how the novel is communicated to us. What differences do we notice in this novel's way of communicating? More description, less dialogue? More interior, less scenic? More overheard, less heard? More private, less public? Do the differences seem fitting?

5. Necessarily last: what about the heroine, her behavior, motives? Compare Anne's responses with Emma's and Elizabeth's. Does our relationship to the heroine seem to have changed, the author's to the heroine, ours to the author? She wrote this book almost twenty years after the first version of *PP*, in the final year of her life. Does the book reflect aging or maturity? Different circumstances? A change in values and tastes? (End of scenario.)

At this point, we are ready to address questions of authorial identity head on. The "why" questions have arisen: Why write? Why write this? Why write differently at this time? General impressions are inescapable. How will we treat them, and what contextual materials will we pause to introduce?

It would be feasible to consider a small photocopied anthology of excerpts from Austen's putative "influences." But to do the job thoroughly would require more time than we can afford. And besides, it is not the coverage that matters. It is the problem of influence in general. How does an author accept and use influences and yet protect her independence and originality? Austen, wrote F. R. Leavis, "in her indebtedness to others, provides an exceptionally illuminating study of the nature of originality, and she exemplifies beautifully the relations of 'the individual talent' to tradition" (14). Against Leavis, we might place Bloom's "anxiety of influence" thesis: a "really strong" author creates by mistaking her forebears and in effect rewriting them. Another critic has said that Austen "began by defining herself through what she rejected" (qtd. in Halperin 36). Perhaps we all define ourselves by what we are not or choose not to be.

Biographical interpreters may take us further than we want to go. Some find the "real Austen" a nature innately ironic, detached, satiric, even sadistic. Persistent satire, they assume, reveals a sadistic streak, and they find confirmation in Austen's surviving correspondence. Shall we assign some of her letters? Marghanita Laski's caution is salutary. She concedes the malicious look of such comments as, "Mrs. Hall, of Sherbourne, was brought to bed yesterday of a dead child, some weeks before she expected, owing to a fright. I suppose she happened unawares to look at her husband." But she warns that the early letters were mostly to her sister and closest intimate:

> [W]e gain the impression of a distinct *persona* established in the relationship between the sisters, a *persona* detached, mocking, above being "put-upon" or taken in, which was not necessarily the *persona* presented by Miss Jane Austen to the rest of the world. (40–41)

Did Austen not "perform to strangers" or did she only perform? The two may mean the same. But if we select from later letters, we can construct very different images of a "real Austen."

> I have the pleasure of writing from my own room up two pair of stairs, with everything very comfortable about me. (5 May 1801)

It seems odd to me to have such a great place all to myself. (15 June 1808)

I am very snug with the front drawing-room all to myself, & would not say "Thank you" for any companion but you. (20 May 1813)

I am now alone in the library, Mistress of all I survey. (23 September 1813)

This is not Elizabeth Bennett speaking, but rather, Jane Fairfax and Anne Elliot. Where is Emma? In neither? In both?

We could also make our construct with the help of a few carefully chosen biographical anecdotes. What about these three?

In November, 1800, Jane was almost twenty-five and had lived all her life at Steventon Rectory. Returning cheerful from a visit, she was met by her mother and abruptly told they were leaving Steventon to live in Bath. Jane, never a fainter, fainted. Her writing almost ceased until, nine years later, the Austen women settled again in Chawton Cottage. Consider Emma's sense of home and its association with creative fancy.

Fixed in a society where only marriage provided a woman with an established home, Austen never married. Of the four suitors we know about, one gave up for lack of money and married "well" elsewhere; one seems to have been a Mr. Collins; one died suddenly. The "last chance" (in 1802, when Jane was Anne Elliot's age) was a proposal by the twenty-one-year-old son of well-to-do neighbors while Jane was visiting. Jane said yes. Then she and Cassandra spent a painful night reconsidering. In the morning she cancelled her yes, and the sisters abruptly drove back to Bath. (Reflect on Emma's persuasions about marriage, compulsive match-making, ignorance of her own feelings.)

Throughout the Steventon years, Austen had written within and for a bright, appreciative family. Her father sought her a publisher. But settled at Chawton, published, recognized as an author, here is how she worked:

[S]he was careful that her occupation should not be suspected by servants, or visitors, or any persons beyond her

> own family party. She wrote upon small sheets of paper
> which could easily be put away, or covered with a piece of
> blotting paper. There was, between the front door and the
> offices, a swing door which creaked when it was opened . . .
> (E. Austen-Leigh, qtd. in Rees 15)

She would not allow the creaking to be fixed; it warned her when
to hide the little pages. She published anonymously, but the
identity of the author was widely known. She spoke affectionately
of her books as her children, but refused to attend literary recep-
tions in the public role of author. Why this intense privacy, this
myth of anonymity, this dogged separation of public name from
private fiction? It is not enough to recall that "professional women
writers were still regarded with suspicion" (Rees 49). It is not
enough to recall the history of privacy, Coleridge's castigation of
"this age of personality," or even the peculiarly private relationship between novelist and novel. There remains something individual in Austen's performing to strangers.

　　If we make such biographical constructs and then "read them
back" into the novels, can we avoid going too far toward seeing
texts as mere "projections," or making "transpositions" back
"along the inverse path" to an authorial personality (Todorov
234–9)? The psychoanalytic biographer might follow such a
course, and seek a "hidden life-myth" or "figure under the carpet." But this is to treat texts merely as "symptomal," and to "re-
constitute a second text articulated on the lapses of the first." I
am trying to avoid two extremes: textual autonomy that denies
the figure of the author any place, and projection that loses the
text in the authorial document. Can we steer between the poles
of rhetoric and psychoanalysis? Criticism, Eagleton argues, can
do "something similar" to psychoanalysis. It can watch not only
"what the text says," but also "how it works" (182). Brooks makes
a sharper distinction:

> It is not that I am interested in the psychoanalytic study of
> authors, or readers, or fictional characters, which have been
> the usual objects of attention for psychoanalytically informed
> literary criticism. Rather, I want to see the text itself as a sys-

tem of internal energies and tensions, compulsions, resistances, and desires. (xiv)

To read this way is to come closer to the author "in the midst of the text." It is to break down the familiar separation between writer and reader. We may see how as we turn to a second reading of *Emma*.

V

In recent pedagogy of composition, we have relearned the inseparability of reading and writing. We read what we write; we write what we read. If so for teaching composition, why not also for teaching literature? Our aim is to become readers as close as possible to the writer composing the text, to discover the author in that process. We need not be unnerved to hear some call this reading or teaching "deconstructively," especially if we discover that we have been doing so naively for years. Barbara Johnson reassures us that "deconstruction is not a form of textual vandalism or generalized skepticism designed to prove that meaning is impossible" [or need not be]. It is a way of reading that "carefully follows both the meanings and displacements of meaning," watches a text work out "its complex disagreements with itself," knows that any text can "signify something more, something less, or something other than it claims to," pays attention to "what a text is doing" (140–1). On second reading, *Emma* becomes for us a work in which a composing agency works out her relations to a heroine and her situation, her world. It may well be that this working out is never quite complete. No human disclosure, no knowledge of or feeling about an other, can be perfected.

A first reading is chiefly conditional on what and when the text discloses. A second reading entertains more of what is not (yet) disclosed, what could be, what might have been. I asked a friend the other day why she was rereading *Pride and Prejudice* for the twentieth-odd time, and she replied, "Out of a sense of the possibility that Elizabeth and Darcy might *not* get together." As readers we play a more active composing role. A greater equality reduces our sense of the author's control (I do not mean of her art) and increases our sense of her as working agency. As Bayley says, we experience "an apparent dialogue between our intelligence and another's" (1). We discover more because we become aware of its being put there, of how it gets there, of what isn't there or might have been.

Since (ideally, at least) we already know or remember "all there is to know," we become more aware of how the author manages knowledge, what is disclosed and when, and what is concealed. And since choices of disclosure and concealment are ethically and socially crucial in Austen's world, they must also be meaningful for a reader in relation to that world and its author. Judgment too is crucial: when to judge, when to postpone judgment or alter it. In second readings we become more aware of our own judgmental behavior and hence of the author's. The author becomes part of the novel's behavior or manners. And when, as with any behavior, we notice a change or a pattern, we ask why. Our question of why confronts the author as a presence in the text.

One suggestive focus for our second teaching of *Emma* is the figure of the kindly, garrulous spinster Miss Bates. We begin with an attentive rereading of her initial portrait (the fourth paragraph in chapter 3), and discuss what we now discover in this remarkable paragraph, having read the novel before, and remembering the author from other texts. We cannot help but "remember Box Hill" from our first reading, but how we remember or misremember will be interesting to test. We inventory the ways Miss Bates would be missed if she were not here. The evolution of her significance is part of the process of the entire novel. Brown constructs this significance from a distanced sociological point of view.

> Miss Bates is perhaps the nearest symbol of Highbury; all classes join and cooperate in her, just as all the gossip passes through her vacant [?!] mind. She is the repository of all that occurs and has occurred in Highbury. Her small apartment

joins the older gentry (the Woodhouses and Knightleys), the new rich (the Coles), and the lower-middle to lower-class townspeople and clerks. She represents Highbury's fluidity and mobility, its tolerance of past and future classes, or part of the sensibility that helped England avoid a French Revolution. (112)

The construct is impressive, but it seems remote from the individual Miss Bates and our relation to her in the text. Moreover, if she really holds so momentous a position, we might well ask why the novel is not called *Miss Bates*. But we could agree that Miss Bates plays a pivotal role in our relations to this world, and that her complicated relation to the author is something whose "working out" we should watch.

Biographers would aid us by telling of possible real-life "originals." The most recent biographer (Halperin 269) even suggests she is Austen's "piece of wistful, ironic self-portraiture," and he quotes, "Her youth had passed without distinction, and her middle of life was devoted to the care of a failing mother, and the endeavour to make a small income go as far as possible." I would challenge any student aware of such a possibility to reread the novel without a new sense of the desperateness of Miss Bates's talk, so near hysteria, so driven by a desire for inclusiveness, for the social space she finds only in talk. This new sense is strong enough to intensify the mood of other things: Elton's emotional violence in proposing; the fearful pathos of Woodhouse's hypochondria and (like Austen's) his obsession with home comfort; the suffering of Jane Fairfax; the distraught restlessness of Frank; and climactically, Emma's own pangs and pain. The book's painfulness grows.

We can't forget, however, that Miss Bates is a figure of what Austen most feared and strove hardest not to be. The phrases most startling to Harding (169)—"she had no intellectual superiority to make atonement to herself, or frighten those who might hate her, into outward respect"—startle us less when they echo phrases from other novels. Of Darcy, early on, Elizabeth says, "He has a very satirical eye, and if I do not begin by being impertinent myself, I shall soon grow afraid of him" (*PP*, chapter 6). In self-defense, Elizabeth uses what Miss Bates lacks. But Miss Bates has what Elizabeth lacks and what the author admires so ambivalently: "she was a happy woman, and a woman whom no one names without good-will. It was her universal good-will and contented temper which worked such wonders." Why should this author reveal such mixed feelings about such a figure?

The very inclusiveness of her interests and her love seems distasteful to the author. Mr. Weston is such another, and earlier novels contain more. The lack of discrimination is also a lack of reserve, an inability to hold oneself back, an obsessive need for society that signals a weakness of private resource. To watch the author impersonating, altering, judging such figures is to sense an unsettled concern for openness and sincerity, a dislike of concealment, but also a distaste for social clutter. Evidently she wants it both ways: openness and discretion, tolerant sociability and private integrity. Don't we all? We learn as the text works out such "complex disagreements with itself."

Miss Bates is presented to us with "her comic aspect foremost." Her absurdity is "explicitly foregrounded." She is the uncultivated bore whose trivial chatter fills (too?) many pages. "She has been described as a bore," writes Elizabeth Jenkins; "indeed, Emma thought so"—we think so, too—we think the author thinks so. But Jenkins outgrows this foreground view:

> [T]he flow of her garrulity has that balanced and dramatic quality which it is stimulating to listen to; the sentences frequently run into each other, but they have that emphatic vividness that shows a mind alive to diverse interests . . . It is not that what she says is ridiculous, but quite the contrary; her comments and remarks are all, in themselves, evidence of a nature that is only trusting and easily pleased; it is simply that they are poured forth in such unstinting abundance that the listener becomes hypnotized in their flow. (301)

I agree. Progressively I appreciate Miss Bates. Only through Miss Bates the storyteller, the repository, am I included in the particularities of this world that Austen's language often excludes. Miss Bates becomes an anti-author. Her talk is created by an author who brilliantly impersonates what she rejects or disapproves of. Parody allows the mature Austen to have it both ways, to include and exclude, to create and exploit the very things she finds ridiculous. We all learn the price we must pay for having Miss Bates there—sympathy and even humility.

Miss Bates is a condition of the author's evolving relationship to her heroine. Such a creation has been long in developing. And here is a fact to teach about any author: the fact of development. As with major events in any lifecycle, each work is a momentous psychological act for an author. Each work, successfully negotiated, prepares for the work to follow. So, says Harding, *Mansfield Park* prepared Austen for *Emma*, "in which a much more complete humility is combined with the earlier unblinking attention to people as they are" (176). In *Emma*, Austen "seems to have taken a great step forward in her confidence as a writer" (Hodge 212). Three novels had been published. Was she growing accustomed to performing to strangers? Any author must. Her niece Anna was now writing a novel with Aunt Jane's wise advice, her mature sense of the genre. The affectionate relations of aunt and nieces remind us that Austen at forty was creating a heroine twenty years younger, with all the quasi-parental distance and intimacy this implies. Her achieved perspective on Emma is well suggested in the letter she wrote to her niece Fanny:

> You are the delight of my life . . . You are worth your weight in Gold, or even in the new Silver Coinage . . . You are the Paragon of all that is Silly & Sensible, commonplace & eccentric, Sad & Lively, Provoking & Interesting.—Who can keep pace with the fluctuations of your Fancy, the Capprizios of your Taste, the Contradictions of your Feelings? . . . It is very, very gratifying to know you so intimately. . . . Oh! what loss it will be when you are married. You are too agreeable in your single state, too agreeable as a Neice [*sic*]. I shall hate you when your delicious play of Mind is all settled down to conjugal & maternal affections. (20 February 1817)

We need not suppose that Emma is "modeled" on Fanny to discover here something of what the novel suggests to us, or why we
share Mudrick's sense that "this time the author is in her novel
and never out of it" (qtd. in Halperin 268).

Why was Emma so long persuaded she would not marry, so
resistant to the idea? The question is now inseparable from many
others. Why was she so long ignorant of her own feelings? Why
a compulsive matchmaker? The question now seems parallel to
the question of why Miss Bates was a compulsive storyteller.
Why, climactically, was Emma so rude to Miss Bates? As Peter
Brooks writes, "No analytic moral logic will give the answer to
the question, why did I behave that way? as it will not answer the
question, how can I be in my proper place? nor indeed the question subtending these, who am I" (32)? He suggests an answer ap-
ropos of another romantic protagonist:

> Julien [Sorel] continually conceives himself as the hero of his
> own text, and that text as something to be created, not
> simply endured. He creates fictions, including fictions of the
> self, that motivate action. The result is often inauthenticity
> and error . . . Julien's fictional scenarios make him not only
> the actor, the feigning self, but also the stage manager of his
> own destiny. (71–72)

Emma would be just such a stage manager, a maker of scenarios.
The role isolates her imaginatively from her world. She projects her feelings into others, thinks herself immune, incapable
of love. She does not yet know herself to be an actor in her
own story.

Her growth teaches her and us otherwise. She evolves from
the vain, foolish manager of the Harriet-Elton scenario to become an unwitting, exploited actor in the scenario stage-managed
by Frank (as almost one in Mrs. Elton's). Coming at last to a
knowledge of her own feelings, she discovers that she is an implicated actor in her own story (every author must). The crisis of
Emma's complicity arrives in the Box Hill exchange with Miss
Bates, her anti-self, a woman who is always a character in her
own story to such a degree that she cannot control the story at all.
Here is how Bayley sums it up:

It is a vital premise of *Emma*, as a novel, that we have to live inside a community, as Jane Austen enables us to live inside the individuals who compose it, and so we have to take the consequences . . . as Emma herself does after her unkindness to Miss Bates. The remarkable force of that event, and the directness of its impact upon us, proceeds from its summation of the whole tendency of the novel—its enveloping intimacy. Jane Austen's art puts us and herself into a community from which there is no withdrawing; a community in which we are entitled to malice, to misunderstanding, to levity, to thoughtlessness—to anything except the right to detach ourselves and contemplate with our author from outside. (5–6)

Contemplative detachment, immunity from feeling and judgment: this is precisely how readers who do not like Austen characterize her, especially nineteenth-century romantics and their Lawrentian descendants. And the half-truth in their complaint helps us realize the achievement, the maturity, of *Emma*.

The decision to execute a novel centered on Emma and to implicate herself in the process was courageous and mature. Austen's relations with her heroines were always complex and personal. They were, says Bayley, "at once a humourous indulgence and a spiritual exercise" (13); I would underline *spiritual exercise* and ask for discussion of what it means. This is especially true of Emma, "whom no one but myself will much like," whom part of the author—how else could she anticipate?—evidently did not much like at the outset. We watch this work itself out. Thus, in rereading *Emma*, we come to feel strongly that "in the midst of the text (not behind it, like a *deus ex machina*) there is always the other, the author" (Barthes, *Pleasure*, 27). And having discovered the author here, we have become implicated familiars, knowing better how to seek her out elsewhere, to catch her in the act of greatness. What better aim could we have in teaching an author? The act of greatness is contagious. Teaching literature is spreading the contagion.

EPILOGUE

An Empty Stage in Half-light. The Stage Manager speaks.

With this account of Emma's stage management, I reach the end of my own in this book of scripts and experiments. The lessons of authority gleaned from the study of teaching an author are many, and they apply to our study of teaching. As teachers, we too are authors, inside the texts we make, and our students try to read us accordingly. Our authority is always inescapable and always problematic. We must make and remake it as we go along in the processes of teaching and learning. Our designs grow and alter as our courses unfold, and as they grow and alter, our roles and styles of teaching vary. Such obligatory versatility is quite confusing at times.

This is perhaps unusually true for us teachers of literature or of "English," who, at present, are somewhat bewildered as to who we are, where we fit in, how many things we can be and do. Edward Partridge asks, "What do we need to know?" and answers, "Everything" (66). But we cannot know, be, do everything; without priorities, what will guide us? Perhaps the only continuous role is that of the Stage Manager, who helps make things (learning) happen, so long as he remembers (like Wilder's Stage Manager) that he must be an actor in his own scripts. The only other universal is the Kimon Rule: if we do not teach our students how to learn, how to become their own teachers, we do not teach them well. Scheffler's Rule Model is our safest guide: learning is a process of acquiring and refining the principles by which we know and understand; the student who learns grows in the capacity for reasoned deliberation.

This is true whether we are teaching the strangenesses of the arts called literature, or teaching the interdisciplines of literature as a humanity, a historical event, a social institution, or teaching the disciplines of reading a complex text in any field.

Otherwise, our choices must be contextual. The kind of course determines them. A kind of course teaches a kind or a way of learning—this is what a discipline is. It should be designed according to its kind. The design of a course determines our choices. The design embodies our assumptions about the orders of its subject and also about what students begin with, what prepares them, in what orders they can best learn. The course's kind and design determine the kinds of questions we emphasize and the ways of answering we teach; otherwise, our pedagogy is uncoordinated. The course's kind and design, and its coordinated questions and answers, determine the modes or styles of teaching we use and when we use them. There are different styles or modes, and each has its part to play according to the context; even the Person from Porlock and the Torpedo Fish have their places.

Perhaps we know, begin to understand, all this. But we cannot carry it out alone. Other teachers can watch us, help us find ways and means. But we will learn to help each other effectively, continuously, only if institutional structures permit and encourage us to do so, and only if our attitudes allow our classrooms to open their doors to colleagues without fear of professional rivalry or excessive anxiety over what grades our performances will receive.

It would help if we could somehow get over the stubborn notion of what we do as "performance." But to some degree this is what it is. You have guessed already a fact about this teacher. He spent his adolescence in and out of the professional theatre, and then turned to teaching as a kindred art. Teaching was performing, and a good performance was all that mattered. Slowly it dawned on him that the close analogy was misleading, damaging. Learners could not be spectators. What mattered—all that mattered—was the learning that transpired. What he had wanted to be all along was not an actor, but a stage manager: not the early Emma kind who imposes her own scripts and mistakes her fancies for her students, but the kind who sets the scene, gets things moving, guides the actions and the players, and then moves out of sight and out of mind.

WORKS CITED

EPIGRAPHS

Broad, William J. "Tracing the Skeins of Matter." *New York Times Magazine* 6 May 1984.

Gurland, Robert H. "Teaching Mathematics." *Scholars Who Teach*. Ed. Steven Cahn. Chicago: Nelson-Hall, 1978.

Nicolaides, Kimon. *The Natural Way to Draw*. Boston: Houghton Mifflin, 1941.

PREFACE

Eagleton, Terry. *Literary Theory: An Introduction*. Minneapolis: U of Minnesota P, 1983.

CHAPTER ONE

Bruner, Jerome. "The Act of Discovery." *On Knowing*. Cambridge: Harvard UP, 1962.

Clinchy, B., and C. Zimmerman. "Epistemology and Agency in the Development of Undergraduate Women." *The Undergraduate Woman: Issues in Educational Equity*. Ed. Perun. Lexington: Lexington Books, 1981.

Freire, Paulo. *Pedagogy of the Oppressed*. Trans. M. B. Ramos. New York: Herder and Herder, 1972.

Hirst, Paul E. "The Logical and Psychological Aspects of Teaching a Subject." *The Concept of Education*. Ed. Peters. London: Routledge & Kegan Paul, 1967.

Martin, Jane. *Explaining, Understanding and Teaching*. New York: McGraw-Hill, 1970.

Passmore, John. *The Philosophy of Teaching*. Cambridge: Harvard UP, 1980.

Perry, William G. *Forms of Intellectual and Moral Development in the College Years*. New York: Holt, Rinehart, Winston, 1968.

Riesman, David, with J. Gusfield and Z. Gamson. *Academic Values and Mass Education*. New York: Doubleday, 1970.

Scheffler, Israel. "Philosophical Models of Teaching." *The Concept of Education*. Ed. Peters. London: Routledge & Kegan Paul, 1967.

Scholes, Robert. *Textual Power*. New Haven: Yale UP, 1985.

Smith, Frank. *Understanding Reading.* 3rd ed. New York: Holt, Rinehart, Winston, 1982.

Whitehead, Alfred North. *The Aims of Education and Other Essays.* London: Macmillan, 1929.

CHAPTER TWO

Bettelheim, Bruno, and K. Zolan. *On Learning to Read.* New York: Knopf, 1982.

Brownhill, Robert. *Education and the Nature of Knowledge.* London: Croom Helm, 1983.

Downing, John A. *The Psychology of Reading.* London: Macmillan, 1982.

Fish, Stanley. "Is There a Text in This Class?" *Reader-Response Criticism.* Ed. Jane P. Tompkins. Baltimore: Johns Hopkins UP, 1980.

Hoffman, Nancy. "Asking Questions in the College Classroom." *Teaching at an Urban University.* Ed. Broderick. Boston: U of Massachusetts, 1987.

Kasulis, Thomas. "Questioning." *The Art and Craft of Teaching.* Ed. Gullette. Cambridge: Harvard UP, 1982.

Scholes, Robert. *Textual Power.* New Haven: Yale UP, 1985.

Smith, Frank. *Reading.* Cambridge: Cambridge UP, 1978.

Tompkins, Jane P., ed. *Reader-Response Criticism.* Baltimore: Johns Hopkins UP, 1980.

CHAPTER THREE

Boulger, James. "Christian Scepticism in *The Rime of the Ancient Mariner.*" *From Sensibility to Romanticism.* Eds. Hilles and Bloom. New York: Oxford UP, 1965.

Brownhill, Robert. *Education and the Nature of Knowledge.* London: Croom Helm, 1983.

Coleridge, Samuel T. *Biographia Literaria. Selected Poetry and Prose.* Ed. Stauffer. New York: Modern Library, 1951.

Cunliffe, Marcus. Foreword. *Gulliver's Travels.* By Jonathan Swift. New York: Signet, 1960.

Davidson, Robyn. *Tracks.* New York: Pantheon, 1981.

Frye, Northrop. *The Educated Imagination.* Bloomington: Indiana UP, 1971.

Irwin, W. R. *The Game of the Impossible.* Urbana: U of Illinois P, 1976.

Le Guin, Ursula K. *The Language of the Night.* New York: Putnam, 1979.

Lewis, C. S. *An Experiment in Criticism.* Cambridge: Cambridge UP, 1969.

Partridge, Edward. "Teaching English." *Scholars Who Teach.* Ed. Steven Cahn. Chicago: Nelson-Hall, 1978.

Polanyi, Michael. *Personal Knowledge.* New York: Harper and Row, 1964.

Ross, Stephen David. *Learning and Discovery.* New York: Gordon and Breach, 1981.

Todorov, Tzvetan. *The Fantastic.* Trans. Howard. Ithaca: Cornell UP, 1975.

Tolkien, J. R. R. "On Fairy-Stories." *The Tolkien Reader.* New York: Ballantine, 1966.

CHAPTER FOUR

Culler, Jonathan. *Structuralist Poetics.* Ithaca: Cornell UP, 1975.

Eagleton, Terry. *Literary Theory: An Introduction.* Minneapolis: U of Minnesota P, 1983.

Gribble, James. *Literary Education: A Revaluation.* Cambridge: Cambridge UP, 1983.

Gurland, Robert. "Teaching Mathematics." *Scholars Who Teach.* Ed. Steven Cahn. Chicago: Nelson-Hall, 1978.

Hawkes, Terence. *Structuralism and Semiotics.* Berkeley: U of California P, 1977.

Iser, Wolfgang. *The Act of Reading.* Baltimore: Johns Hopkins UP, 1978.

Vygotsky, L. S. *Thought and Language.* Trans. Hanfman and Vakar. Cambridge: M.I.T. Press, 1964.

CHAPTER FIVE

Barthes, Roland. "Literature as Rhetoric." *Sociology of Literature and Drama.* Eds. Burns and Burns. Harmondsworth: Penguin, 1973.

Bate, W. Jackson. *Samuel Johnson.* New York: Harcourt Brace Jovanovich, 1977.

Eagleton, Terry. *Literary Theory: An Introduction.* Minneapolis: U of Minnesota P, 1983.

Fleishman, Avrom. *Fiction and the Ways of Knowing.* Austin: U of Texas P, 1978.

Goldmann, Lucien. "The Moral Universe of the Playwright." *Sociology of Literature and Drama.* Eds. Burns and Burns. Harmondsworth: Penguin, 1973.

Hoover, Kenneth. *The Elements of Social Scientific Thinking.* 2nd ed. New York: St. Martins, 1980.

Malraux, Andre. *Anti-Memoirs.* Trans. Kilmartin. Naw York: Holt, Rinehart, Winston, 1968.

Nisbet, Robert. "Sociology as an Art Form." *Sociological Perspectives.* Eds. Thompson and Tunstall. Harmondsworth: Penguin, 1971.

Siebenschuh, William. *Fictional Techniques and Factual Works.* Athens: U of Georgia P, 1983.

Spring, David. "Interpreters of Jane Austen's Social World." *Jane Austen: New Perspectives.* Ed. Todd. New York: Holmes and Meier, 1983.

Trilling, Lionel. *The Liberal Imagination.* Garden City: Doubleday Anchor, 1953.

Wain, John. *Samuel Johnson.* New York: Viking, 1975.

White, Hayden. "Historical Text as Literary Artifact." *The Writing of History.* Eds. Canary and Kozicki. Madison: U of Wisconsin P, 1978.

CHAPTER SIX

Cohen, Ralph. "Innovation and Variation." *Literature and History.* Eds. Ralph Cohen and M. Krieger. Los Angeles: Clark Library, 1974.

Fowler, Alastair. "Periodization and Interart Analogies." *New Literary History* III (1972).

Scholes, Robert. *Textual Power.* New Haven: Yale UP, 1985.

White, Hayden. "The Problem of Change in Literary History." *New Literary History* VII (1975).

CHAPTER SEVEN

Berry, Francis. *Poetry and the Physical Voice.* New York: Oxford UP, 1962.

Cardinal, Roger. *Figures of Reality.* London: Croom Helm, 1981.

Dewey, John. *Intelligence in the Modern World.* Ed. Ratner. New York: Modern Library, 1939.

Easthope, Anthony. *Poetry as Discourse*. London: Methuen, 1983.

Eliot, T. S. *Selected Essays*. New York: Harcourt Brace, 1950.

Frost, Robert. "The Figure a Poem Makes." Preface to *Complete Poems*. New York: Henry Holt, 1949.

Grigson, Geoffrey. *The Private Art*. London: Allison and Busby, 1982.

Hawkes, Terence. *Structuralism and Semiotics*. Berkeley: U of California P, 1977.

Hoffman, Nancy. "Asking Questions in the College Classroom." *Teaching at an Urban University*. Ed. Broderick. Boston: U of Massachusetts, 1987.

Hollander, John. *Vision and Resonance*. New York: Oxford UP, 1975.

Kasulis, Thomas. "Questioning." *The Art and Craft of Teaching*. Ed. Gullette. Cambridge: Harvard UP, 1982.

Kintgen, Eugene. *The Perception of Poetry*. Bloomington: Indiana UP, 1983.

Kristeva, Julia. *Desire in Language*. Trans. Gora, Jardine, Roudiez. New York: Columbia UP, 1980.

Nemerov, Howard. *Figures of Thought*. Boston: Godine, 1978.

Poulet, Georges. "Phenomenology of Reading." *New Literary History* I (1969).

Riffaterre, Michael. *Semiotics of Poetry*. Bloomington: Indiana UP, 1978.

Skelton, Robin. *Poetic Truth*. London: Heinemann, 1978.

Stauffer, Donald. *The Nature of Poetry*. New York: Norton, 1962.

Styan, J. L. *The Dramatic Experience*. Cambridge: Cambridge UP, 1965.

Whalley, George. *Poetic Process*. Westport: Greenwood, 1973.

CHAPTER EIGHT

Burns, Elizabeth. *Theatricality*. London: Longman, 1972.

Edens, Durer, Eggers, Harris, Hull, eds. *Teaching Shakespeare*. Princeton: Princeton UP, 1979.

Elam, Keir. *The Semiotics of Theatre and Drama*. London: Methuen, 1980.

Esslin, Martin. *An Anatomy of Drama*. London: Temple Smith, 1976.

George, Kathleen. *Rhythm in Drama*. Pittsburgh: U of Pittsburgh P, 1980.

Hyman, Stanley. *Iago: Some Approaches to the Illusion of His Motivation*. New York: Atheneum, 1970.

Styan, J. L. *The Dramatic Experience*. Cambridge: Cambridge UP, 1965.

Wilder, Thornton. Preface to *Three Plays*. New York: Bantam, 1972.

CHAPTER NINE

Arendt, Hannah. *The Human Condition*. Chicago: U of Chicago P, 1958.

Barthes, Roland. *The Pleasure of the Text*. Trans. Miller. New York: Hill and Wang, 1975.

Barthes, Roland. *S/Z*. Trans. Miller. New York: Hill and Wang, 1974.

Bayley, John. "The 'Irresponsibility' of Jane Austen." *Critical Essays on Jane Austen*. Ed. Southam. London: Routledge & Kegan Paul, 1968.

Brooks, Peter. *Reading for the Plot*. New York: Vintage, 1985.

Brown, Julia. *Jane Austen's Novels*. Cambridge: Harvard UP, 1979.

Chatman, Seymour. *Story and Discourse*. Ithaca: Cornell UP, 1978.

Eagleton, Terry. *Literary Theory: An Introduction*. Minneapolis: U of Minnesota P, 1983.

Foucault, Michel. "What is an Author?" *The Foucault Reader*. Ed. Rabinow. New York: Pantheon, 1984.

Gilbert, S. M. and S. Gubar. *The Madwoman in the Attic*. New Haven: Yale UP, 1979.

Gordon, George. *The Lives of Authors*. London: Chatto and Windus, 1950.

Halperin, John. *The Life of Jane Austen*. Baltimore: Johns Hopkins UP, 1984.

Harding, D. W. "Regulated Hatred." *Jane Austen: A Collection of Critical Essays*. Ed. Watt. Englewood Cliffs: Prentice-Hall, 1963.

Hodge, Jane. *Only a Novel*. Greenwich: Fawcett, 1973.

Jenkins, Elizabeth. *Jane Austen*. New York: Farrar Straus, 1949.

Johnson, Barbara. "Teaching Deconstructively." *Writing and Reading Differently*. Eds. Atkins and Johnson. Lawrence: U of Kansas P, 1985.

Laski, Marghanita. *Jane Austen and Her World*. New York: Viking, 1969.

Leavis, F. R. *The Great Tradition*. Garden City: Doubleday Anchor, 1954.

Lukacs, Georg. *The Theory of the Novel*. Trans. Bostock. Cambridge: M.I.T. Press, 1971.

Mudrick, Marvin. "Irony as Discrimination." *Pride and Prejudice*. Ed. Gray. New York: Norton Critical Edn., 1966.

Ortega y Gasset, Jose. "Notes on the Novel." *The Dehumanization of Art*. Garden City: Doubleday Anchor, 1956.

Rees, Joan. *Jane Austen: Woman and Writer*. New York: St. Martins, 1976.

Rousseau, Jean Jacques. *Confessions*. Trans. Cohen. Baltimore: Penguin, 1953.

Scholes, Robert. *Textual Power*. New Haven: Yale UP, 1985.

Todorov, Tzvetan. *The Poetics of Prose*. Trans. Howard. Ithaca: Cornell UP, 1977.

Trilling, Lionel. "Manners, Morals, and the Novel." *The Liberal Imagination*. Garden City: Doubleday Anchor, 1953.

Trilling, Lionel. Introduction to *Emma*. By Jane Austen. Boston: Houghton Mifflin, 1957.

Watt, Ian, ed. *Jane Austen: A Collection of Critical Essays*. Englewood Cliffs: Prentice-Hall, 1963.

GENERAL INDEX

INDEX OF
TEACHING TEXTS